Screwed
Without
Intercourse

Screwed Without Intercourse

Gordan Stevens

authorHOUSE®

AuthorHouse™
1663 Liberty Drive
Bloomington, IN 47403
www.authorhouse.com
Phone: 1-800-839-8640

Published by AuthorHouse   08/10/2012

ISBN: 978-1-4772-5696-1 (sc)
ISBN: 978-1-4772-5695-4 (hc)
ISBN: 978-1-4772-5697-8 (e)

Library of Congress Control Number: 2012914213

To my Wife,
The One that has made
all of my dreams come true,
and to my Daughter,
who has made me so proud.

FOREWORD

The story you are about to read is true.
Every word of it.
The names have been changed.

Fiction can be fun. This story is not.

❊ CHAPTER I

I was a student at a state university in town, working towards getting my baccalaureate degree in Nursing. I lived on my own, working 40 hours on the weekends at a local hospital as the office clerk in the X-ray department.

I began to date one of the employees in medical records, an oriental woman named Mindy. Mindy was completely Americanized; she had no accent from her heritage. When I met her, she was separated from her husband, Bob, of 15 years.

They had been apart for 3 years, and Bob had given Mindy $0.00 in financial support for their three kids. This was a necessity for Bob, since every extra dollar he earned went to feed his methamphetamine habit. His crank habit also happened to be the reason that Mindy told him to hit the road; they filed for bankruptcy protection that year. It was 1989.

When we started dating, Bob had been out of Mindy's life for so long that all three children constantly asked Mindy when dad would be around again. Unbeknownst to either of us, he would suddenly decide he wanted Mindy back as soon as he found out she was dating someone, and he was willing to confront any man who stepped in his way to take back his property. Who would have guessed that Bob would have the law on his side?

One night while Mindy was over at my place, someone knocked on the door, loudly and forcefully. Instantly, both of them knew who was at the door. It was Bob. Instead of opening the door, I called 911 trying to avoid a confrontation.

Now, mind you, Bob was a Phillipino, small in frame, topping the scale at 150 pounds, maybe 160 after a meal of pizza & beer, and standing around 5 foot 3 inches. I was a champion swimmer as a youth, weighed in at 175 pounds, and stood 5 foot 11 inches. The notable size difference made me the obvious victor in any hand-to-hand combat that may take place. So why call 911? Why not just go out and kick the hell out of him? I had my reasons.

Mindy had told me of the violent rages Bob would go into when under the influence of crank. And he was a Vietnam veteran, exposed to all the death & destruction that went along with it. Active duty equals Combat. Since I was never enlisted, I had no active service time, let alone active duty! Thinking that Bob was highly trained in combat and had killed before, I was quite reluctant to confront the smaller man, despite my size advantage.

By the time that the police arrived, Bob had already left my property, and was driving down the street. I was on the phone with the 911 dispatcher, alerting her that the police had just driven by Bob in his car. They turned around and apprehended Bob. He had an open container in the car, a can of beer. The police took him downtown.

However, after holding the intoxicated driver overnight and listening to his terrible story, about how I was stealing his wonderful wife away from him and destroying their wonderfully tight family, the Valley City police department released him. No DUI, no charges at all. It wasn't his fault. He had a right to protect his property, according to the police. And Mindy was his property.

This happened two more times, the last being on New Year's Eve of 1990. Each time, I remained inside, trying to avoid a confrontation. Each time, the police spoke to Bob, but after learning of the situation, took his side and filed no assault charges against him. Their advice to me: quit seeing Mindy. She's married to him, and that's the way it is. Even my dad told me it was time to stop seeing Mindy, insisting that this relationship was going to lead to no good.

But the police and my dad were wrong. Something special had started between Mindy and I, and we knew we had a future.

Our lives on this planet are finite; there is an end to them. Some of us search for happiness our entire existence while others seem to run right into it. When I first saw Mindy, she was dressed in a long, blue velvet dress. The kind that hugged her small frame, showing all the curves that drive most men crazy. Hell, even gay men were turned on by her! I was not immune to her beauty.

But there was something special between us. Mindy felt it too. Many people don't believe that love just happens. Some say that love must grow and flourish and be nurtured to be anything worth keeping. We did not have a chance to work at loving each other; we fell in love the moment we first met.

And then on April 7, 1990, the unthinkable happened.

Mindy came over that night to spend some time with me. After going to sleep early that evening, we were awakened by a phone call. It was Bob.

"I want you out of that house and back home with your family where you belong," he told her. "If you're not home in 30 minutes, I'll come over and smash the windows and slash the tires on his truck.

But Mindy wasn't afraid of him. Her only concern was that I not be involved in this crap anymore. So she got up and left. But Bob showed up at my place anyway.

He pounded on the front door at around 2am. I jumped out of bed and grabbed the first thing I saw; a buck knife folded up on the dresser. "If he's gonna slash the tires on my truck," I thought as I hastily headed to the front door, "then he's gonna be armed with a chain, maybe a bat, and/or a knife." Armed and ready, I went out through the front door. Directly in front of my house was a street lamp, which shined a bright light on the entire driveway of my corner house.

"4 times the police have been called because this asshole is assaulting me. 4 times they have let him go. How many more times will this be allowed to go on?" I asked myself.

"None," was my answer. What ensued was a fight to the death between two men: one scared to death, the other 'amping' out on crank.

Since it was 2am and the streets were deserted and quiet, I remember my voice echoing off the surrounding houses. I walked hurriedly up to my assailant, shouting, "Why did you come here?"

I saw a flash of light in Bob's hand, and the thought that he was armed as well gave me all the reason I needed to go on the offensive. Something happened to me in that next moment.

It was as if something had caused me to leave my body and become a third party in what was about to occur. Like an out-of-body experience reported by patients who have been legally dead and are then brought back to life, I could see myself as he and I came together. The anger welled inside me, an anger I'd never before experienced. Like an animal that has been backed into a corner, the feeling of dread that I must either fight or be beaten, kill or be killed, I must do for myself what the police would not.

I kicked him in the midsection, causing him to bend over at the waist. Without giving him a chance to react, I swiftly and forcefully brought the buck knife in my hand down on his back.

On the first strike, he twisted as the knife entered between the 5th & 6th rib. The 4" long, ¼" thick blade snapped off in his chest, sitting ¾" from the tissue that surrounds the heart. I continued to stab at him as he twisted around in circles like a tornado dance performed by an American Indian. What I didn't know was that I no longer had a 4" blade at the end of my knife; it was now only about ½" long.

As he spun around, I slashed frantically with the knife in my right hand while holding the lapel of his leather jacket behind his neck with my left hand. With each rotation, the material bunched up more, and after 3 rotations, I had to let go.

He fell to the ground in the crawl position, suddenly realizing something is in his chest. Before he could think about his next move, I let loose with a kick to his chest, much in the same way a football place-kicker would kick a football in the attempt of a 60 yard field goal.

He flew through the air as he saw the kick coming and jumped upward. As my kick connected with his chest, he was already on the way up by his own power, and the added force from the kick lifted him completely off the ground, as if he'd sprung from a springboard.

He landed at the foot of the streetlight. On all fours, he grabbed his chest and saw the blood for the superficial wounds on his chest and stomach where the random slashings had made contact.

"My God, what have you done?" he looked up and asked me.

As he said this, the out of body experience ended. Like a vacuum sucking a large amount of dust from the air, I felt my soul reenter my body, and I gasped,

"My God, what <u>have</u> I done?"

I looked at my hand that held the knife. The blade is broken off. Now all the events appear to be in slow motion. Bob looked up at me, and said,

"Man, somebody's gotta call 911."

"No shit someone better call 911," I yelled at the top of my lungs. The sound of my voice echoed down the empty street like I was in a cave. One of the calls to 911 that came in shortly after that was from 3 blocks away!

I stepped back, now getting my feet back under me. The 'return' of my soul into my body was complete, which is the only way I can describe it, and now reality was setting in.

I looked at my hand with the knife, and thought to myself, "The blade is gone. Where the hell's the blade? And the blade is half closed. Why is it half closed? Oh, because it stopped on my pinky finger. Christ, I'm cut!"

The blade had closed on my finger, cutting to the bone. In fact, the bone was broken from the force that was exerted by the slashing blows upon my assailant's back. The wound would require 17 stitches to close. The fracture of the metacarpal bone of the 5th digit went unnoticed until sometime later.

Upon noticing that my finger was cut, I went into my house to call 911. I left him lying on the sidewalk, tending to his wounds. After calling 911, I went back out to check on the jerk, starting to realize now that he may die. As I entered the doorway to exit my house, the car that he had arrived in drove off.

"The man just got stabbed once, and he's driving down the road somewhere. How amped up is this guy?" I thought as I watched the taillights disappear around the corner.

When the police arrived, I was up front about everything that had happened. Over the police radio, it was heard that he had shown up at the hospital; the same one that I worked at. I was never read my rights because I volunteered all the information I gave. The officers never asked me if my assailant had a knife.

I don't recall ever seeing a knife anyway. I saw a flash of light, but was that a knife? Or was it a wristwatch band? Or a ring? It could have been anything. I looked at myself. "No wounds except the one inflicted by my own knife," I thought to myself. Was it possible that I had escaped any injury from his knife, if in fact he did have a knife in his hand?

When the officers arrived at the hospital, no knife was found in his car, but a baseball bat was in the back seat. Bob's condition was critical. Although only one wound was serious, that wound included a knife blade very close the heart. The X-ray department where I worked took the X-ray that showed the blade perched next the pericardium, the tissue that surrounds the heart.

After learning that no knife was found in his car, I was arrested. As I was being placed in the back of the squad car to head off to a different area hospital to have my finger stitched up, Mindy drove back up.

Terrified, she ran from her car to the window where I sat, handcuffed behind my back in the patrol car.

"Don't make it any worse than it is, Mindy," I yelled to her. "He came at me, and I had to kick his ass."

Mindy broke down. This could not be happening. The guy she was just getting to know and really like was going off to jail because her punk ass estranged husband wouldn't leave him alone. Now I'd fought back like anyone would in the same situation. She pleaded for the police to arrest Bob, regardless of the seriousness of his injuries. He came here to my house, she stated. It was 2 in the morning when he arrived. I had tried everything to get Bob off my case. And now it had come to this.

Due to the seriousness of the attack, I was put on temporary leave without pay from my job at the hospital. I'd been working there for 4 ½ years, and now overnight, because I was faced with living or dying and decided I wasn't ready to lay down and die, I had nothing. No way to support myself. No way to feed myself. No way to live.

When Mindy offered me to come and live with her, I accepted.

When I arrived at Mindy's house for the first time, I thought I'd taken a wrong turn and arrived at a dump. 2 broken down cars littered the driveway. A large pile of broken cement pieces lay on the front lawn near the front door. The yards were overgrown with weeds and tall grass. In the back yard, washers and dryers and refrigerators sat rusting and taking up space. Most of the windows in the house were broken, including the sliding glass door. Inside it was generally clean, but in dire need of paint.

I had the cars hauled away cheaply, made a couple of trips to the dump which included all of the broken cement pieces, painted the rooms inside the house, cut the grass and trimmed the hedge and the palm trees in the front yard. And I found a used glass dealer that came in and replaced all the windows that were broken for under $300. The children were 14, 11, and 8, respectively.

Debra, the oldest and only girl, was just at the age of that a young lady starts the search for her identity, with peer pressure being the most important issue in her life.

Sam was the youngest, a very talented young artist who could pencil draw figures such as the Teen Age Mutant Ninja Turtles to a tee! Sam would like nothing better than for his mom and dad to be back together, but he seemed to be okay with me living in the house and being his mom's boyfriend.

Kyle was the middle child. He was the only child that didn't understand the incident, and blamed me for all of it. We stayed away from each other, and my time living at the house went by without incident between the two of us.

✳ Chapter II: The Trial

The trial came in December 1990. I had no past incidents to prepare me for what was to come. In my eyes, I had done nothing wrong except protect myself, so I refused to pay money to an attorney. "Our justice system will prove I was in the right," I thought to myself. I obtained a public defender as a lawyer. That was the second biggest mistake in my life.

The 'dumptruck', so named by repeat offenders because she looses many easy cases, was a pathetic piece of work, interested more in how much cleavage she could show in the courtroom than in how well she could defend the charges against one of her clients. My biggest mistake was believing that the justice system would protect me from wrongful imprisonment.

Before the trial started, the D.A. offered me a deal of 7 years in prison. I had many things I wanted to tell this jackass, but I simply said "No."

During the trial, the public defender decided to stipulate with the District Attorney that the victim in this case, Bob, was in fact on methamphetamines, also known as crank, as noted by the drug test taken at the hospital when he arrived after the incident. My blood test came back negative for any drugs, of course. I was in a 4 year university, studying to be a nurse.

By 'stipulating' that Bob was on drugs, no doctor took the stand to explain how violent and radical being high on methamphetamines makes a person; the first evidence of a lousy attorney. And it all happened so fast, without the public defender even asking me if I was okay with the motion, that it was done and forgotten before I could utter a word. My attorney assured me that this would not make any difference in court.

The lady who lived next door to me was the only witness. She was waiting up for her daughter to arrive home. When she heard the commotion out front, she looked out her window that overlooked the street. She then went to her bedroom in the back of her house to call 911.

While dialing, she testified, she heard someone yell, "Some one better call 911," but the voice was not that of her neighbor, the defendant, but of the victim, Bob. My attorney was so lame that she didn't even bring up the fact that a man who has a punctured lung from a stab wound can't catch his breath enough to yell, let alone yell loud enough to wake someone three blocks away!

It came out in the trial that Bob was a Vietnam Veteran. There he worked in the Medical Corp, working behind the lines with injured soldiers. As I heard these words coming out of the lips of Bob, I suddenly realized that this tiny piece of shit wasn't anything to be afraid of.

But now it was too late. Without an attorney who was good, the evidence was against me. But I didn't know that at the time. I was naïve, to say the least. I was a fool, to be more precise. I'd been brought up to believe that the law never punishes anyone who is not guilty of the crime for which they stand accused.

The rest of the evidence was clear. I admitted stabbing Bob in self-defense. The question was—did I have justification for acting the way I did? That was the question before the jury.

Under questioning, I admitted to seeing the flash of light that gave me reason to believe we were both armed with a knife. I described the many times Bob had come to my house previous to the night of my arrest, and how the police had refused to charge him with a crime. Each time I made a comment, the D.A. would object to the way I answered, stating it was subjective, to which the judge would 'sustain'.

As the trial progressed, it came into evidence that a knife had been found at the hospital where Bob had driven himself after being stabbed. This knife was found only 3 days after the incident occurred. Not a broken knife, but a full sized, 'Rambo' type knife with a serrated edge and the little container in the handle. The groundskeeper at the hospital was brought onto the stand, and testified that the knife was found in the bushes near the emergency room entrance, and that the knife was not rusty, but looked like it had only been there for a few days at most.

Even though this knife was found and presented to the D.A.'s office, the D.A. did nothing to see if it belonged to Bob. No fingerprint lifting was performed on the knife. Nothing. No attempt whatsoever to see if this knife belonged to Bob, which would indicate that Bob, not myself, was indeed the aggressor and perpetrator of the incident.

The D.A. went a step further in his closing arguments, calling my dad, a life-time member of a federal government agency in law enforcement, a liar.

"Surely, he would say whatever would be necessary to keep his son out of jail," he said.

During the time of the trial, I was in a daze, unable to really grasp the severity of everything that was occurring in the courtroom. All of the motions and rulings that I had no idea why or what they were for led to confusion on my part, and instead of asking for a clear explanation of what was, or had, happened, I relied on my attorney to do what was right for me.

In my attorney's closing argument, she jumped up and down like a little schoolgirl, trying to get her point across that if I hadn't acted the way I did, I would have been the one stabbed and not Bob. After seeing her performance during her closing statement, I thought her theatrics were the right touch to a close case. Boy, was I wrong.

❈ Chapter III: The Verdict

The trial lasted 5 days, the jury deliberated for 3. On that third day, January 8, 1991, they reached a verdict: Guilty.

> Guilty of Attempted Murder in the second degree.
> Guilty of Use of a Deadly Weapon.
> Guilty of Grave Bodily Injury.

I was taken into custody immediately. My mother sobbed at the news that her son was to be locked up, to which I screamed at her,

"Don't you cry! Don't you let that bastard win anymore than he has already. He played the system and won, and don't let him win anymore."

I shot a quick glance at Bob. I was sure that he'd be gloating heavily on the upcoming incarceration. But he wasn't gloating, not even smiling. I never found out why.

And so on January 8, 1991, I went to jail.

I was arrested right there in the courtroom, handcuffed by one of the bailiffs and removed from the courtroom via a back door. The back door led to a long hallway that attached all of the courtrooms to each other, for easy removal of new convicts to the jail across the street.

After the conviction, I stayed in the city jail until my sentencing hearing one week later. When the week had disappeared, and it went by unusually fast, the sentencing hearing date had arrived. It was at this point that things took an upturn in my favor, if there was any 'Up' to my current scenario.

The sentencing phase was different than what many of us are used to. I had always thought that if you're convicted of a crime, then you're a criminal and you belong in jail. The defense, of course, was arguing for probation as an alternative to jail for me. I had no prior criminal convictions for any violent offense, I was in college, I'd found a job at a home improvement store after the incident, and I was from a good family with Christian values.

The prosecution, of course, argued for the maximum of 7 years in prison, dismissing all of the evidence presented in the trial that Bob was the aggressor and all of my attempts to get the police to stop Bob's violation of my rights.

However, the judge saw something in the evidence, or maybe in myself, that gave him cause to hand down a sentence much different than what anyone in the courtroom that day expected. The judge gave me a 90 day observation period prior to his official sentencing. Let me explain.

A 90 day observation is a period of time that a prisoner is incarcerated at a state prison, and the prisoner is observed for his behaviors and attitudes. It also includes a multitude of testing by psychologists and counselors.

For myself, I would spend my 90 days at Inacia City State Prison, also known as the state hospital for the criminally insane. After the first sentencing hearing, I spent around 10 more days at the county jail until I was transferred to the county jail south of Valley City, the Valley City Men's Ranch, also known as 'the Ranch'. This was the holding place for all prisoners going either from the jail system to the prison system or vice versa. It was located roughly 40 miles out of town, in the middle of cow fields and corn stalks. I did not welcome the isolation.

❖ Chapter IV: Imprisoned

I had no intention of allowing my new circumstances to change me into the criminal mentality that now surrounded me. From inside the walls of detainment, I kept myself busy writing letters to Mindy and my family. The first month was the hardest. This was my first time locked up with criminals. And my mom had mentioned to the guards that she was afraid that I would be suicidal. Thanks, mom. That's not something to say to jail guards. The regulations on inmates now required that I be placed on suicide watch. And you know where they put suicide watch prisoners? On the psychiatric ward of the jail.

At that time, I didn't know about my mother's comment to the guards. I'm sure she meant well in her sweethearted attempts to protect her son, without being aware that she was actually making things worse. When I arrived on the jail floor where I was to be staying, I immediately realized that most of these inmates were nuts. With my training in Psychiatric nursing and my time as a psychiatric technician at a local psych hospital, I was very aware of schizo patients, and they were all over the place on this floor.

I dated the letters I sent out to Mindy and my family, hoping someday to make use of them to show that I was not the horrible person depicted by my conviction and ensuing incarceration. What follows are the contents of those letters.

Day 17: January 24, 1991

It took me 16 days to stop pinching myself and realize that this was not a dream. This was reality. Up to this point in time, I had spoken to family members on the phone and had some visits through plexiglass, but I found the ability to write a letter almost beyond my ability to concentrate; for all practical purposes, I was living in what could only be termed 'Hell'.

As I sat in the jail cell, trying to keep my sanity about me, I used up the time by writing letters and songs, hoping to play the later for Mindy some day when I was free. I silently cried inside when I received a letter from my probation officer that a large number of letters from friends, employers, doctors, nurses, educators, and family members had been submitted to him as letters of reference. After the verdict, my lawyer had requested that my parents get as many letters as possible from those that knew me, showing a positive person who deserved something less than jail time. These letters would be presented to the presiding judge of my case at the time of sentencing.

I took advantage of getting out of my jail cell as much as allowed. One day, I played basketball in the outdoor recreation area, a game of 2 on 2 basketball. Although my team lost, I enjoyed myself—it took my mind off my troubles for a while, which was a good thing. I needed the diversion. And I needed the exercise.

I seemed to be doing pretty good at keeping myself busy. I read the paper everyday when we were out of our cells for dayroom (TV's and phones) time, and I played solitaire and read the Bible when we were locked down for 23 hours. Now that the first couple of weeks had passed, it was almost—that's almost—bearable.

As the days went by, I found writing to be easier, and it seemed to be good therapy for me. The pencils they sold us (in commissary) were short, so they couldn't be used effectively as weapons, so short in fact that I had to take a break every 30 minutes or so because my hand kept cramping as I struggled to hold on to the tiny utensil. My back kept hurting, too, since I was forced to sit on the edge of my bed and write on the table right next to it. At least I had the bottom bunk.

My cellmate appeared to be nocturnal. When I woke up around 3:30 one morning, he was at the door just staring at the empty room before him. I was glad not to be lost like him. I don't think he even knew how to read, so I wasn't worried that he'd read any of my letters or mail. I thought he was okay, until I found him trying to pull out one of his teeth. He said it was loose and was ready to come out. He acted like it was no big deal. All I could think was, "God help me if my teeth start to fall out!" How disgusting. He slept all the time, probably a side effect from the Haldol they gave him for his obvious psychiatric problems.

I hoped to get a picture of Mindy soon. I hoped to see her face in the morning and at night before I went to sleep.

I continued to feel lucky for the family that was so supportive of me through this trying time. Many of the other inmates received zero social visits and never used the phone. These same people often stayed in their cells when we were allowed out for dayroom privileges. One morning, when the guards announced outdoor recreation time, only 5 out of the 32 inmates on my floor responded. They instead wanted to stay in and watch the television.

I was surprised at how easily I could sleep. The noise in the cement jail room was pretty constant during the day, but the mattress wasn't too uncomfortable. The units that housed the inmates consisted of two levels of cells, a top floor and a bottom floor. Both floors shared the dining and TV area. Being up on the second floor, I figured nothing very exciting would happen in the unit. Well, so much for uneventful days.

One night a new inmate was brought into our floor. All night long he kept yelling from his cell, "I'm sorry, I won't do it again." Over and over. The dead quiet of the unit made his voice reverberate off the walls and echo throughout the cell. It continued on for most of the night. I think I fell asleep around 4am.

16

In the morning before breakfast is served, the guards do a role call, to make sure no inmate has escaped from this 4th floor, completely made of concrete and solid steel, sarcophagus. When role call is performed, the guards open all of the doors on the top or bottom floor, and all of the inmates on that level would step out of their cell onto the blue line on the floor 2 feet in front of their door.

On this particular day, the bottom floor's doors opened, and the inmates stepped out and were counted. Then it was the top floors turn. The doors opened, and I stepped out to be counted.

As I stood there, from the cell 3 doors down, this inmate came bursting out of the cell, ran around the corner of our balcony heading straight for the stairs. But instead of taking the stairs, he jumped over the end of the balcony and landed flat on his back on the concrete below!

The second floor was made for security so we were up about 25 feet. When the inmate hit the floor, I saw blood splatter all over the window next to him. I figured he was dead. But my instinct was to help him.

As I started to walk towards the stairs, the inmate in the cell next to me said, "Don't. Just stay there. They'll think you had got something to do with it." He obviously knew what he was talking about, so I stayed put.

The guard taking role call walked over to the lifeless body, leaned over him, and took out his radio to call for medical assistance. The guard's body language told me that all he could see in this lifeless blob on the ground was a whole bunch of paperwork, explaining what happened, why it happened, and how it could be prevented next time.

After calling for assistance, he told us all to return to our cells. Man was I freaked. I couldn't believe what I had just seen. At least, what I thought I had seen.

I could see though the small glass on my cell door that the attendants were picking up the injured inmate, but I couldn't see the window where the blood had splattered. No sooner had the inmate been taken away than the guard called for role call again. As I stepped out, I looked over at the window where the blood had covered the inside.

Nothing.

Not a drop of blood anywhere. I'd have sworn that I saw blood go all over that window. But there was none. And the guards didn't have time to clean up what I'd seen. Later during lunch, I asked another inmate that could see the whole thing from his cell if the blood had been cleaned off by the guards.

"Blood?" he asked. "Didn't see that. Just that asshole cutting into our TV time." Such human compassion. So I was led to believe that my mind did some overtime imaging and no blood ever did splatter the window. That's wild. I guess that is what psychologists talk about when they say that 4 people on 4 corners of an intersection can witness an accident and all 4 will give different accounts of what happened. None of them are lying; people just interpret events differently when they are under stress. And I was under a lot of stress.

I prayed that the judge would see the truth in this case, and be fair in sentencing me. I thought about Mindy constantly.

Day 38: February 14, 1991

My family visited me once a week while I was at the city jail. However, after the sentencing hearing, and my subsequent move to the Ranch, the visits were short and far between due to the distance they had to travel to see me. I continued to adjust to life in jail, amazed at what occurred and what was allowed.

My time at the Ranch was the most unpleasant of surroundings up to this point of my incarceration. Convicts were housed in 12 or 14 bed dorms, fed in the cells on plastic trays, and allowed out for recreation time only one hour every 48 hours. As the days passed at the Ranch, I realized that this is the way jail should be.

In my new cell at the ranch, I found myself getting along fine with the other guys. The food there sucked, totally opposite of what the inmates at the city jail had told me about it. The city inmates had assured me, while downtown, that the food at the ranch "was 100% better than here." Of course, those guys didn't know what good was, so I wasn't terribly upset that their tastes were quite different from mine.

One of the classes I'd taken in college was Basic computer programming, and I took the time I had now to actually write out an entire program. I would need a computer in order to troubleshoot any programming errors, so I sent the whole written code home. By the time I was released from incarceration, the Basic language was practically obsolete. I had actually thought that I would be interested in spending time on it once released. Looking back, what was I thinking?

I also mailed a few songs that I had written and the pictures that my family had sent to me. I didn't want to have them taken away from me in the process of being transferred to Inacia City. I asked that they return them to me at Inacia City after I arrived there.

I won't lie; it wasn't easy being there at the Ranch. Talking to my family and Mindy on the telephone made writing long letters a mute point. Sitting in that jail cell with 12 other inmates, all of whom were back in jail and on their way to prison for at least the second time, I felt threatened and uneasy.

Even in this situation, I knew I'd come out of this place ahead of the game. Somewhere deep down, seeing the other guys I was incarcerated with and how they didn't have what I did in the way of support, led me to realize the advantage I had to get me through this chapter of my life.

While I was incarcerated, I continued to read the bible I was allowed to have in my jail cell at the City Jail and at the Ranch. I found no solace in the scriptures; by now, the Old Testament was seeming too violent for my tastes and the new testament seemed magical, almost phony. In all the religious teachings I'd had as a child, I never took the time to read the bible and think about its words for myself.

The following are some of the passages that I found most humorous, and I decided to send them home for Mindy to laugh about too. Sometimes, as in the first quote from Genesis, it was just the wording that made me laugh. But most of the passages did not make sense to me. Having been raised as a Christian, I was surprised at what I read.

Genesis 2:24

"Therefore a man shall leave his father and mother and be joined to his wife, and they shall become one flesh."

Deuteronomy 25:5-10

"If brothers dwell together, and one of them dies and has no son, the widow of the dead man shall not be married to a stranger outside the family; her husband's brother shall go in to her, take her as his wife, and perform the duty of a husband's brother to her.

And it shall be that the first born son which she bears will succeed to the name of the dead brother, that his name may not be blotted out of Israel.

But if the man does not want to take his brother's wife, then let his brother's wife go up to the gate of the elders and say, 'My husband's brother refuses to raise up a name to his brother in Israel; he will not perform the duty of my husband's brother.'

Then the elders of his city shall call him and speak to him; and if he stands firm and says, 'I do not want to take her,'

Then his brother's wife shall come to him in the presence of the elders, remove his sandal from his foot, spit in his face, and say, 'So shall it be done the man who will not build up his brother's house.'

And his name shall be called in Israel, 'The house of him who had his sandal removed.'"

I laughed every time I read it! Finding phrases like that while I read through the Old Testament shocked me. "What a trip," I remember saying to myself, "to find such stuff in the Holy Bible."

Luke 14:25

And great multitudes went with Him (Jesus). And He turned and said to them, "If anyone comes to me and does not hate his father and mother, wife and children, brothers and sisters, yes and his own life also, he cannot be my disciple."

Without realizing the implication of this passage, I was again shocked. I came to realize that it is implying that to worship Jesus and God, one must put all others below the Lord and God.

Romans 12:20

Therefore if thine enemy hunger, feed him; if he thirst, give him drink; for in so doing thou shalt heap coals of fire on his head.

I did not agree with this passage at all. I was still stuck on the "Eye for an Eye" passage in previous scriptures.

My mother had a live-in maid who helped her with the 6 foster children now in my parent's care. Gloria was the second mom to those six kids, and a close friend of the family's. She had taught my brother, sister, and me to swim when we were in grade school, so her history with my family went back quite a ways in time.

Later in her life, Gloria had become a prison guard at one of the oldest prisons in California, South Central. While there, she was injured by an upset visitor of an inmate; she caught the visitor trying to smuggle dope into the prison in his shoe. The 6 foot 7 inch visitor picked up Gloria and body-slammed her on the concrete floor, breaking a disc in her back and putting her on permanent disability.

After my conviction, Gloria did what she could to alleviate my mother's fears about the system. Unfortunately, what she told my parents turned out to be incorrect. She wrote a letter to me, explaining that my wonderful defense attorney, the "dumptruck", had called my mother and suggested that I not receive any correspondence from Mindy while on the 90 day observation at Inacia City.

Simply put, Ms. Dumptruck felt that any letters to or from Mindy, which would be noted in my prison file, could influence the judge to believe that I did not feel any remorse for what had occurred. Just for the record, I did not feel any remorse for my actions. I still believed that I had been wrongly convicted and that I defended my life as any person has a right to. Unfortunately, that's what most incarcerated people say, so I couldn't successfully argue my case with any of the other inmates!

Day 39: February 15, 1991

I was transferred to Inacia City State Prison on this day to begin my observation period. I had all kinds of preconceived ideas of what prison would be like. I had hoped it would be less horrible than I'd imagined. I quickly realized that most of my fears were indeed unfounded.

When I first arrived at Inacia City, all of the inmates that had traveled with me from the Ranch were taken into a processing area, stripped naked, searched for contraband (the usual "Bend and Cough"), and given a new set of clothing. Being that we were all on the Reception side of the prison, we were given green jeans and white Tshirts, and a lousy pair of shoes.

The green clothing identified us as "Transferrees" as opposed to the other prisoners that were serving all of their sentence at Inacia City. Those prisoners were dressed in blue shirts and blue jeans. Thus, I came to know the different parts of the prison as the "Blue Side" and the "Green Side." These two types of prisoners were, for the most part, kept separate from each other.

Dressed in our wonderful green clothing, we were then led down a long hallway to the unit where I would spend the next 3 months. This unit had three floors to it, with a 24-man dorm on the bottom floor, and 2 bed cells on the rest of the bottom floor and on all of the top 2 floors.

When I was placed in my cell, another prisoner was already in there. He had been there for almost 2 months. There was an upper bunk and a lower bunk, a toilet and a wash basin. And a window that didn't close too well.

My cellmate was friendly, and told me he was locked up for violating his parole on drug charges. We got along quite well, and he gave me some good advice for staying out of trouble while I was locked up.

Day 40: February 16, 1991

The next day, a man named Tom came to my cell door, the guard opened the door, and I was allowed to step out of the cell, unsupervised and uncuffed, to talk with Tom. I had no idea what was going on. As it turned out, Tom was the husband of a woman that I worked with at the hospital back home. He was locked up for drug charges as well, but had been in Inacia City long enough that he was in good standing with the guards and was allowed to approach me in my cell.

Tom wanted to make my time here as easy as possible, knowing that I was a first-timer and not really clear of what to expect. He gave me some shampoo, soap, instant coffee, and tobacco. (I would find out very soon how truly valuable coffee and tobacco were in prison.) He also had a number of novels for me to read. "It really helps pass the time," he told me.

Like my cellmate, he advised me on some rules to follow to stay out of trouble. His advice and gifts surely made the first days of this experience in Inacia City safer and easier.

I sat in my cell with my cellmate all day, beginning the first of many novels that Tom had brought me. I was under the impression that the only times we were allowed out of the cell were for breakfast and dinner, which meant we were taken to the mess hall to eat and then returned to our cell. Lunch was a sack lunch served in our cell. After being led to the chow hall and having dinner, I was back in my cell, with the assumption that the day was over.

However, it was a Saturday, and at about 7pm, the inmates were allowed out of their cells for "social time", to visit with others and play cards in the mess hall. The T.V. was on, but the ambient noise from all of the talking was so loud that the T.V. was inaudible. I had a table that I was able to write at, and I'd brought along some of my instant coffee that Tom had given me. Not being familiar with the other inmates, I sat at the table I was at for the next two hours and wrote down all I could think of about my new surroundings.

Day 51: February 27, 1991

By this time, I had completed the psychiatric testing for my 90 Day observation period. The questions they asked were pretty strange. For instance, 1) Had I ever been engaged in unusual sexual activity? (Of course, I answered yes!); 2) Did I know that people were following me? (false); and 3) Was I very emotional? (true). They asked so many questions (567) that I was left wondering what they could decipher from the answers, even with my knowledge and experience in psychiatric nursing.

During this time, I had received a letter from my "new" attorney, an appeals lawyer, stating that he was sending a private psychiatrist to perform his own testing on me, in addition to the testing already performed by the prison psychiatrist. His name was Dr. L., and I looked forward to seeing him, and getting started with his tests.

The prison also gave me (all inmates get it) an IQ test. Two of the 30 guys in our 'class' rated at 133—yep, I was one. Not bad. The psychologist who told me my score said he was impressed. I was hopeful that this would be passed on to the Judge. However, I knew that the test was false. I had seen all of the questions on the test before, so I knew the answers.

I tried to keep my brain active by reading the novels I had received from Tom. I read a number of novels, most of which did not thrill me, but did keep in me engrossed enough to pass the time effectively. Actually, they were all hard to put down. What else did I have to do with my time?

In one of the books, I learned that Richard Wagner was Hitler's favorite composer. That's something to keep quiet about! I'd always been proud of Wagner, and finding out this fact, I was a little disappointed. But Wagner didn't choose Hitler—Hitler chose Wagner.

The reason I mention that was because my mother's maiden name was Wagner, and she had thought, incorrectly, that her side of the family had descended from Richard Wagner's lineage.

I watched as much news as I could on the chow room T.V. and I tried to keep up on the war in Iraq, but for lack of continuous information, I didn't know what was happening over there. We didn't get newspapers.

Day 56: March 4, 1991

A few days ago, I went out to the yard when the inmates are allowed even more "out of cell" time, with the opportunity to lift weights, play basketball, etc. When I arrived back at my cell, my cellmate was gone. He approached me today on the yard. I was stunned because I thought they'd sent him home! They just moved him.

The next day I got another cellmate. He was talkative, and basically a nice guy. He was one of the people caught in the system, unable to escape. He kept violating his parole for some stupid reason. (I came to realize that about 65% of the people in prison that I met were locked up for some parole violation.) His name was Gus, and we got along great. He was to be going home in a couple of weeks, and he said something stupid will happen within 60 days and he'll be locked up again. If he is in a store, and the store is robbed, he could be arrested for "being at the scene of a crime", a parole violation. What Bull Shit. That's the system we've come to know. Gus was the first person I'd talked to about Mindy. Oh, yeah, Mindy . . .

All this time away from her hadn't changed the way I felt. By this time, I'd come to terms with my feelings for her. All my adult life, since after the motorcycle accident I went through in February 1983, I had searched for that woman who would love me as much as I loved her. I was lucky enough to have loved 3 other girls. All those girls were potential wives, but none of them could love me the way I needed to be loved. Looking back, I probably scared the hell out of them with my talk of marriage after only a short time of dating them.

I had never set a standard on the girl I would marry. I knew that the 'perfect' woman was not real, but a fantasy. Age never mattered to me with the women I dated until Kari (a wonderful 42 y/o I dated from Serenity River College when I was 20) asked me to marry her. It was then that I realized there was a limit.

When I thought about Mindy, about what had happened, and what I should do with her, I came to realize that by continuing to think with my brain, and not my heart, I'd always have a reason not to marry her. I believed in Mindy. She put something in me that I had never received from any girl before—she gave me that 'loved' feeling. I didn't want to try to find someone else who would feel this way about me anymore. It had taken me 7 years to find her. And I wanted to start a family. Now. Whether my parents agreed with my decision, I felt like I was getting old. Hell, my parents were married when they were 20 or so. I was almost 30, and I could feel the years slipping away.

Although I had many reasons not to marry her, and my dad and I had talked about those reasons, I had one reason to spend my life with her—I loved her. And it wasn't a kid love. It was a love that I had never doubted, unheard of with most of my other girlfriends. We had started off as friends, and that simple fact is what made our relationship work. I wasn't trying so hard that I scared her away.

I knew I'd disappoint my dad with my decision, but I had to stay with the feelings I had for Mindy. I didn't know how my parents had gotten together—he'd never told me—but if he could remember back to those days before he had proposed to my mom, I thought, he might also have battled with himself over whether mom was the girl for him. I'd come to see that my dad and I thought in the same manner, and I was proud to be his son because of the great upbringing he had given me. I hoped that he would see my love for Mindy, and give me his blessing in my decision. I wanted to bring up a child or two with Mindy, and show them all the love that he had given me.

I had told the probation officer, "My dad and mom are the best parents anyone could ever have." It was my hope that they would understand where my thinking was coming from. Of course, that meant reneging on my promise to them to walk away from Mindy, but I couldn't walk away from her. This time, I had to 'play the hand out, and go all in.'

The time seemed to go pretty fast while at Inacia City, since I went outside to the yard every day. It was about 6 acres with 2 gun towers overlooking it. I worked out every other day with the weights, and I had decided to start jogging around the field to improve my stamina. I didn't want to get too buffed up, though, and end up looking like a convict! I jogged around the field 15 times today, which was the equivalent of 5 miles. My legs felt it, too!

In the physical they gave us upon entering Inacia City, I was shocked to find out that I weighed 190 Lbs! And it was all muscle. My belly was firmer than it had ever been. I thought I only weighed 175 Lbs at the most.

I learned something interesting about being sentenced to prison. After 6 months or more in the state penitentiary, upon release the inmate receives $200 cash to help him/her out on the street.

I was pretty concerned about what would happen to me when I was released from incarceration. I couldn't live with my parents, as they had foster children, and a convicted felon wouldn't fly with the Social Services. I couldn't see anyone giving me a job. I'd have no money, and I'd be on probation or parole, depending on how the sentencing went. The unknown of how I was going to fit back into civilian life scared me the most at that point in time.

I couldn't believe the way the guards allowed the inmates in this prison to scream to each other. All night long, they sang their stupid rap songs about smoking crack and stealing and running around in the gang back home. All the inmates seemed to know at least 20 of the others in the prison. It was just one big, happy, extended family for them. It made me want to puke!

I hoped that my mother's faith in God would return. She had lost hope after the trial, and it upset me to think that, after the religious teachings that she had allowed me in my youth, the event the led me here had caused her to turn away from the church.

If my family had come to visit me, the prison policy was that visitors could not wear blue jeans or green slacks, or white shirts. Those colors were the color of the clothes that inmates wore, and they wouldn't want to look like an inmate.

It took a money order from my parents to get "Canteen" funds on my prison account so I could buy snacks and other items while locked up. Funny how such a trivial thing was so important to me at that time.

It was hell in there, but I saw why so many prisons are over-crowded. Instead of what I'd heard before, about a roof overhead, 3 meals and clean clothes, the reason inmates were happy here was because 'all my home boys are here.'

What was wrong with these people? I cherished my freedom more than ever at that point.

Day 57: March 5, 1991

I was awakened early this morning by the wing guard. With some help from my friend, Tom, I was to start working Monday through Friday as a painter. I was on a crew of 10 inmates, working on the 3rd floor of the new "X" wing, which was to house inmates that were diagnosed with the AIDS virus, exclusively. The AIDS patients had already moved into the first floor cells. As odd as the inmates in the general population in my wing were, these inmates were some real weirdos! Unfortunately for me, the job only lasted two weeks, since I came in late on the work, and the crew I was on completed the 3rd and final floor of the "X" wing in rapid time.

I enjoyed the painting job because it made the days fly by and it kept me off of the yard. Any time not on the yard, I felt, was time that I was not at risk of getting jumped or into trouble with another inmate.

Day 65: March 13, 1991

Good news was brief and almost nonexistent for me while at Inacia City. I was hoping for a visit from my parents at some point, but I received a letter with news that because they were foster parents, they had a file with the Department of Justice, and that would make the clearance time longer for them to be approved for a visit. Par for the course, I thought.

This day also marked the receipt of a notice that my parents had put "money on my books," meaning I could go to the canteen and purchase some luxury items. In prison, that means soda cans, shampoo, and tobacco. Canteen was on a set schedule for each different wing of the prison, and my wing's day was Wednesday. It was unknown if the system would process the payment fast enough for me to be able to use it on March 20, 7 days away.

Day 66: March 14, 1991

I finally saw Dr. L., the psychiatrist that the appeals lawyer had hired to give me private testing for additional leverage in my sentencing hearing. Dr. L. was very amiable, and started off the testing by giving me a blank piece of paper, and asking me to draw him a picture. I drew a picture of a dream I had while I was on morphine at UCD, after my motorcycle accident and near-death experience. It was an 'Adam & Eve' scene, with me and a woman walking naked through the Garden of Eden, with wild animals gazing at us. There were snow capped mountains and a waterfall. I found it a challenge to illustrate the water accurately since I couldn't add any color, and my artwork never had been much to boast about.

After that, the psychiatrist took a history of me. He asked how I liked myself, how growing up was for me, and how school was. He inquired when the first time I had sex was, if I had any lasting relationships with girls (Mindy and Kelli were the only two that lasted more than 3 months) and how many close friends I had (just one—Tony).

He then asked me some questions, like "If you were lost in the forest, how would you find your way home?" and "If you found an envelope with an address and stamp on it, what would you do?" They were all open questions, ones that I had to answer with something other than a 'Yes' or 'No'. Then the questions became definitions of words. Most I knew, but I was stumped on a few of them.

The next test was an inkblot test. Although I knew about this type of test, I did not know what the cards would look like. For each card, I had to come up with 2 different figures that I saw in the ink blot. Some of them looked pretty violent. Despite my actual response to the doctor, I saw a cat flattened out by a steam roller, an F-14 in Iraq, a man shot with a shotgun, and the world blowing up. The colors were supposed to make me think "violent" thoughts (black, white, and red). So I tried to come across as mellow as possible, thinking about how to appear nonviolent to him. What I really told Dr. L. I saw on the inkblots I had forgotten by the time I returned to my cell!

After the testing, I knew it was now just a matter of time before I found out which direction I was headed, the county jail or state prison.

This was my 28th day at Inacia City. I hated it more each day, with the feeling of humiliation growing as I dealt more with the group of people I was imprisoned with.

I hadn't received a letter from my parents for about a week at that point in time. I assumed they were pissed at me because of what I had stated in my previous letter to them, regarding my feelings for Mindy. I had tried 3 times to walk away from Mindy, but my heart kept telling me that my life was destined to be with her.

How could my parents, lawyer, or judge of my case expect me to stop loving her? When I had promised to them that I would leave Mindy, I had every intention of doing so. But love was not a switch; at least it wasn't for me. My heart didn't work that way. I wasn't cold enough for that, nor had I been brought up that way. The only way to really love someone was to accept the person they were.

Today was rainy, and loving the rain, I did my best to keep from getting down. My cellmate obtained a job in the kitchen, so I was alone from 3 to 9:30 every night. I was trying to get a job in there as well, but 90 day obs inmates usually don't get jobs, so the short painting job was a real bonus. I guessed that the prison system wanted to make us suffer so we realized our mistake. It was my firm belief that this place was hell enough without that!

I received a letter from someone on the "outside" almost every day. That made me feel pretty special. Many of the inmates I spoke to were happy if they received one letter a month. The little things, like that, kept my spirits up through those trying times.

I had received a few letters from the appeals lawyer. One was a transfer of Power of Attorney from the Dump Truck that the county issued me in my defense (my public defender), another was to let me know that Dr. L., would be visiting me here (a little late since I'd already seen him), and one which is the legal contract of him now being my attorney. I prayed that he could find something to appeal and have the judgment against me overturned.

In need of anything to get me out of my cell, I signed up for church services that were held every other night. I wasn't sure what to expect from a church service in prison. I thought we'd to go a chapel, right? Nope. Just to a classroom. And then the service was black gospel. I hated it, and despite the thought of sitting in my cell instead, I decided not to go back. I had to sit for an hour and a half on that first and only church service, listening to the 'Amens' and the 'hallelujahs'. Oh, well—another lesson learned.

I'd been reading some novels given to me by Tom, and I read 'The Exorcist' in two days. I was hurrying through to see how it ended, and I arrived at page 386, read to the bottom, and then started reading the next page. Oh, No! I exclaimed, as I realized that the next page was 403! Yep, I missed the entire end of the book. That was the second novel I'd read that was missing a page or pages at the end of the story! What luck—another lesson learned.

Besides all the lessons I was learning in a short period of time, I was doing just fine. I hadn't had any problems, and my cellmate continued to give me good prison advice. Among other things, he told me not to be stingy with my coffee and tobacco. Yea, I smoked 1 or 2 cigarettes a day, but it was only because of boredom. I assured myself that I would quit when I was released.

Day 69: March 17, 1991

It never stopped amazing me how ridiculous and uneducated the inmates around me were. They believed almost anything they heard, almost relishing in the excitement of news about another inmate in another prison who had been told by another prisoner that such and such had occurred, regardless of how asinine the news was. I wrote letters to my parents to help me cope.

It was raining again, so, needless to say, I was cooped up in my cell. This made the day drag out terribly. I would usually have been out on the yard from about 9am until 2pm, but it was cold enough in my cell. They did allow any inmate that wanted to go out to the yard on a rainy day to do so, but I'd be damned if I was going to voluntarily go out in the rain! I had been able to go out yesterday, since I didn't work on the weekends. I had worked out on the weight set(s), and I felt a bit sore this next day.

Yesterday's yard time was quite illuminating for me, and I wrote down some comments made by the ICAA—Idiot Convicts of America Association, just so I could tell my parents about some of the asinine things I was told in the big house.

ICAA Comment #1: "Don't lift weights using your arms and then your chest on the same day because you want the oxygen you inhale to only go to one part of your body."

This ICAA member was trying to tell me that I shouldn't curl weights (a bicep exercise) and use the bench press (a peck and shoulder exercise) on the same day. He tried to convince me that the first muscles you exercise on any given day require more oxygen than the other muscles of your body. In this instance, he implied I would strain my shoulders doing bench presses since I had started the day with curls.

I didn't tell him I was a nurse, and I didn't tell him he was an asshole either. But I really wanted to.

ICAA Comment #2: "Vistaryl isn't for that—it amplifies the effect of the drug you are taking with it."

This ICAA member, with tattoos all over his body from neck to fingers to waist (& probably below), tried to tell me that he was being given motrin and vistaryl for his back pain. I asked if the motrin made him naseous, because that is what vistaryl is for—it's an antiemetic; it keeps you from puking! He looked at me and said,

"No man, that ain't what vistaryl is for. You don't know."

I just walked away. He was too stupid to know 2 plus 3, let alone understand what I based my knowledge of drugs on.

I didn't tell him I was a nurse, and I didn't tell him he was an asshole either. But I really wanted to.

ICAA Comment #3: "These 90 day ob(servations) people got it rough. If the judge tried to give me a 90 day ob, I'd tell him to give me 2 years state time instead. I'd have the prison term knocked out with no problem."

Another goon, talking out of his rectal orifice. Like most of the prisoners, they had no life outside of these walls, and I was so afraid of what awaited me when I was released.

I didn't tell him he was an asshole. But I really wanted to.

And now for the category of "Things I could have complained about, but who would have listened?"

I tried to cut my hair on my own on this day with a razor, but I didn't have a mirror, and I just couldn't get the reflection in the window of my cell door to give me a clear enough picture of where I needed to cut. So I stopped before getting started. It was getting rather long at this point, but I refused to allow anyone in this or any prison system to cut my hair. The only thing that they knew how to do was crew cuts and "shave the head bald." No thanks.

Although the food is mediocre around here, it would be nice if they gave us time to finish. Last night they gave us about 3 minutes to eat dinner. I was really pissed. They won't let you take food back to your cell, so what you don't finish, you have to throw away.

The temperature of my cell was frigid at times. The previous week, everybody on the first floor was complaining of how cold the cells were. The upper floors were warmer because heat rises. But this week, the cells had been fine, temperature-wise. They had hot-water pipes in the walls between cells, and that was how they warmed the cells at night. The only problem was that the guards had to decide that it was actually cold enough to warrant the heat being turned on. By now, I'd been coughing for a couple of weeks, and it was still lingering.

Although I had received a receipt for money my parents sent to the prison for canteen use, the prison system had not yet placed that figure on my account, so I had to be satisfied with the $9.70 on my books, which transferred with me from the Ranch, when canteen occurred on Wednesday. They didn't answer my original question, "Is the money sent in by my parents available for me to use at canteen this week?" Let's see—another lesson learned.

All that I needed was some deodorant, toothpaste, conditioner, and playing cards. Anything left over would be used to buy a real soda. It had been 63 days since I had a coke. That would be nice to get, if the prison did acknowledge that I had the money on my books. I had written a letter to them, and they had replied that yes, I did have $9.70 on my account, but I would have to wait until this week to use it. Oh well, that's prison.

Today was day 31 at Inacia City. I wondered how long I'd be left in that scummy place? I wished I had some idea. I wondered if my parents had heard anything from my attorney? I didn't know what to expect anymore. Prison was stupid, filled with ignorant people with less drive than a worn-out transmission. When I listened to their pathetic stories, I wanted to scream. But I couldn't, and I didn't. Patience is a virtue . . . .

I saw Nancy & Tom through the yard fence today while out on the yard. They were on a conjugal visit. Despite all that he'd done for me, I felt troubled when I saw them together. This was prison, and in my beliefs, when you are in prison, you shouldn't get to have sex with your wife. That's part of being locked up. You're a prisoner and have lost that and many other rights. There I was, incarcerated, a prisoner, trying to understand how our society could think that somehow by allowing conjugal visits it would keep the family unit strong for that prisoner and his family. I just didn't get it. The ongoing onslaught of "Prisoner's rights" in this place never failed to make my stomach wince in agony.

Day 70: March 18, 1991

The day had started out much like any other day in prison. But it soon turned out to be different. Before breakfast, I received notification that no work detail would be done today. I wasn't told that the painting job was over, which it was, just that there was no work today. You'd think that would be the message, "The job you had is over." Instead, I was left thinking that I had a day off and I'd return to painting tomorrow.

So after breakfast and the morning role call, I headed out to the yard for a run around the yard and some weight lifting. It became interesting pretty quick.

On this day, I witnessed a crime that left me baffled. I couldn't write about it, since all of my mail was screened by prison officials, and if I had written the story describing what I saw, I knew that the guards would question me. And I already knew what happened to those who talk while in the general population.

As I reached the yard, I remembered how open the field was and how threatened it made me feel.

"If you get into trouble, you'll blow any chance you have of getting probation after your 90 day ob is over," I thought to myself as I started to jog around the 440 yard field.

I had completed my first lap and had passed the last of the four corners of the square track when I noticed three men standing on the handball court, about 20 feet from the track that I was running on. One was talking to the other, and the third was standing back just a bit from the other two.

Just as I was about to go past the three, the one standing back sucker-punched one of the other men. The man's head snapped back from the blow to the jaw, and his head bounced off the handball court as both of the other men slowly walked away like nothing had happened.

I stopped running, remembering what my cellmate had told me.

"If any trouble goes down around you, don't run away. The guards look for inmates running away as the culprits of any situation, and they may take a shot at you. And if the guards in the towers say 'Everybody down', get down on your belly. They won't play with you. If you even look like you're gonna get up before they say 'Clear', they will shoot you."

I kept walking, waiting for one of the two tower guards to notice the man laying on the ground, probably with blood pooling around his head. I wanted to assist the guy, but remembered the advice back at the city jail when the crazy guy jumped off the second balcony: "Let it go."

I hadn't walked more than twenty steps when the call came out.

"Everybody down."

I actually chuckled to myself as I laid down on the track. I was practically the last man on the field down on the ground. It was as if every other prisoner on the yard knew it was coming too.

The guards brought out a stretcher and carried the guy off to the infirmary. I couldn't believe what I'd witnessed, and I was shaking inside knowing that any inmate could be the target of such violence.

I went back inside at the first call, and my cellmate was already there. I explained what I'd seen, and my experienced cellmate told me not to repeat that story to anyone.

"If you tell that to the wrong person, you'll be as dead as this stick. You can't tell who's a homey of who in here, so forget what you saw." And he didn't say 'Whom'.

Good advice, I thought. And I followed it. I never wrote about the incident until I decided to tell this story in this book. I remember all these details because it was such a haunting sight to see such raw violence directly in front of me.

Day 71: March 19, 1991

Today my old cellmate Gus was suddenly and unexpectedly removed from my cell, and transferred to another facility. I thought I would have at least one night alone, but instead I came back to my cell after spending time on the yard, laid down, and before dinner, a nice guy named Gary was put in the cell with me.

Gary was also a 90 day ob, and this was his first time in prison, too. He had a wife and a four year-old girl, and it made me feel better to be able to help someone else get through the rough time one has when he first arrives in the system, just as Tom and Gus had helped me out when I arrived here. The first week is tough until you get used to the routine. Gary was dealing with some depression, and I offered as much advice as I felt was appropriate. I knew I didn't have most of the answers to being here. Hell, I was still learning on a daily basis! Hopefully, I was able to give him at least a little peace of mind in those first days at the prison.

Day 72: March 20, 1991

Yesterday, I went to the doctor for this stupid cough I'd had for longer than I could remember. They diagnosed me as having Bronchitis. They started me on a decongestant and ampicillin four times a day, and after only one day, I was already feeling like the cough was going away. I didn't cough that morning and I coughed very little the previous night. I was surprised how quickly the medication had helped me.

Day 76: March 24, 1991

On the 38th day of my 90 day observation, I was getting used to the daily routine. I didn't like it, but it was better than I had planned for.

A couple of weeks ago, I had applied for a job as a clerk in the wing office of the intake unit I was being held in. I'd figured because I was a 90 day ob, I wouldn't be getting a job there, but it was worth a try. Anything to get out of the cell for a little more time.

Day 77: March 25, 1991

Despite what I'd been told by other inmates, I did get the job as a clerk in the office of the intake unit. 2 other inmates worked with me, and I soon had new privileges not allowed to all prisoners.

As a clerk, I was allowed to have some of the office supplies in my cell, such as ink pens of different colors, erasers, and extra pencils. I was given a work-pass and was able to take messages to the other wings, unsupervised by guards. I proved my usefulness to the intake unit CO by cleaning out the filing card index that consisted of inmate names that were no longer in the wing. I then typed a list of all the inmates from the large ink board where the names, cell numbers, and CDC numbers were written for easy reference. I crosschecked the list the next day to make sure that each inmate had a card in the file. The CO seemed to be mildly impressed.

Day 78: March 26, 1991

During the time I had in the office, I was allowed to use the typewriter to write letters to my family. I was allowed to use the colored paper in the office for these letters, which I thought was a nice change from the old, drab white paper that I had been using.

This was another good day, with the day going by quickly as I brought the office up to standards of efficiency. The other inmates and the guards were amazed that any convict would go to all the trouble that I did to get the files updated, the drawers organized, and the job descriptions filled out and on the wall. I guessed they didn't get too many inmates who cared about what they did, whether they were paid for it or not.

Today was day 40 in Inacia City. I looked forward to the day I would go see my counselor for a final counseling session, and then it would only be a matter of days before I returned for my sentencing hearing. I had not heard anything from the appeals lawyer as to what he had been doing on my case. I wanted to know if he had contacted my parents about anything regarding my case.

As mentioned before, my days in prison were flying by, now that I worked every day. As a matter of fact, that is what those of us that worked in the office talked about on a regular basis. There were four people who worked in the office now, three of those being from the green side. The other member was an innate from the blue side, where Tom was. We all got along pretty well, and the time out of the cell made it so it did not seem like being in a prison at all. I was able to run up and down the hallways of the prison, delivering messages to other wings, and I had a pass that I wore on my shirt all day so everyone knew that I was out of my cell with the authority of the officers in charge.

I'd given up on having any visitors here at Inacia City. Even as a clerk, I was unable to find out anything on the background check that they had told me was holding up the visits from my parents. I was doing fine, and I had decided by that time that I really didn't want them to come and visit me in that sick hell hole. It was pretty disgusting, and I would rather see them when I arrived back in Valley City at the Ranch, even thought that was pretty disgusting too. It was just closer to home.

I hoped that I'd return soon to the Ranch and then I wouldn't have to deal with this CDC system anymore, if the good lord was willing.

I had been taking the antibiotics and decongestant prescribed for me by the Dr., and my cough was almost completely gone.

My room was much warmer for the last week or week and a half than it had been. I guess they either decided to turn the heater on again after shutting it off for the spring, or they were able to fix it after it broke. No one ever leaked word to me about why the rooms were so cold, but now they were just the opposite. The heat was almost too much, but I decided the heat was better than the cold any day.

Day 82: March 30, 1991

I attempted to fill my days with constructive means, and not allow my mind to go to waste. I witnessed strange behavior by the other inmates, and kept mostly to myself.

The prison was a haven of drug dealers, drug users, thieves, and punks, beyond what I could have described as the all-too-friendly society of mundane substance in both function and populace for the improvement of the soul and mental health pertained herein. In other words, the place sucked!

I had started welcoming new comers to the place by saying, "Good Morning, and welcome to Hell." It wasn't really that bad, but only because I worked so much to pass away the days. For those that thought of the place as their home, I'm sure they loved it. For the other few like myself, I couldn't imagine how they were able to cope without finding a job to keep their mind occupied.

I did not see the justice in my incarceration. Of course, I didn't want to, but that was beside the point. I was starting to think about the trial more now than I had before. I kept trying to understand why the judge would be so one-sided? He seemed to have been on Bob's side during the entire trial. Was the judge a veteran? Was that why he made Bob the innocent victim? Or was it because Mindy and Bob were still legally married?

My dump truck lawyer failed to ask the judge if he had ever been divorced. Or if he had ever found out his wife or girlfriend was messing around on him. Any of which would have made this case a conflict of interest for him. For me, I just wanted this to be in the past.

Today was day 44 at Inacia City. I decided to ask one of my past mentors, a professor at CSU, Valley City, to talk to his daughter, who was the supervisor of her nursing shift at Central City Hospital, about the possibility and plausibility of a job for me there after my release. I didn't make it a habit to ask for favors, but I figured the time in my life had come when it had become a necessity.

I wrote to my parents and informed them of my letter to him, and that if he contacted them about visits at the jail, or about past employment, to make sure he was given the information he needed. I didn't want to sound pushy, but if I had a job upon release from this system, it would be that much easier to stay out of trouble. And it would make relocation easier, also.

I needed to get out of Valley City, I thought. I had wanted to do so for quite a while, and the reason for staying was school and work. I thought that it would be very appropriate to put some money into Tom's account after all the nice things he had done for me. It would only skim the surface of how much his kindness really meant to me.

I really enjoyed my new job as a clerk. The time seemed to be going much faster than when I was painting; I think because (A): the job was more interesting; & (B): the hours were longer (8am, right after breakfast, to 2:30pm). I usually ended up typing a couple of schedules every day, for the kitchen crews that changed just about every day due to releases to other prisons of inmates working in the kitchen. So my typing skills were at least being kept up. And I had access to a pen instead of a pencil. I hated writing in pencil. The lead would go dull, and I didn't have a sharpener in my cell so I have to rub it on a piece of paper to get the lead to a fine point.

I tried to get a second shift as the PM clerk. That would have allowed me 14 hours out of my cell each day. The night clerk was leaving that week, and I had been "buttering up" the officer in charge of the office in attempts to get that job. I hoped to get it, as working all day would really make those next couple of weeks, probably my last here, go by very fast.

Day 84: April 1, 1991

Tiring of sending the same mundane letters to my parents, I came up with this letter to convey current events and add a little humor to my situation.

Dear Mom & Dad,
I'm not sure just what to say,
    Because nothing has happened worth mentioning today.
So I've decided to write and let you know
    That I'm not doing awful, just doing so-so.
Today is a Monday, and we know what that means
    It's been more exciting, for some reason, it seems.

It has something to do with a sure, simple fact
 That today is the first of month four, that's exact.
The jokes have been flying all over the place
 And I have been lucky, not one in my face.
I've listened to others and the pranks they have played
 And I'm glad for the progress in mind that I've made.
I remember the crazy old tricks that we played off
 Some were quite funny, and some made us scoff.
The trick I remember most clearly, this time,
 Is the one that ol' Scotty played on us, the slime.
He switched all the salt with the sugar, one morn
 And when dad spiced his cereal, a monster was born.
It was so funny, those long years ago
 The laughter, the feelings, the simple "ho-ho's".
And time has not faded the memories of such,
 No other family has ever had loving so much.
I'm so glad to be a part of this team,
 This family's so special, that's what I mean.
But now I am talking, and I might start to cry,
 So I'll change the direction: OK, mom, Sigh.
I enjoy my new job, the time goes by quick
 I've finished my pills, and now I'm not sick.
With everyday, I wish I were home,
 Instead I am here, and I feel so alone.
I'm not that unhappy, I'm not all that glad,
 I'm not very gentle and I'm not even mad.
I just keep on counting the days that I spend,
 And hope with some prayers, that soon this will end.
How are you, and dad, and the rest of the group?
 I hope you are well, no one suffers the croup. Oop!
I forgot for a second, that the 'P' is not heard,
 I only remembered as I spelled out that word.
No, wait, I'm confused . . . is it that little term?
 Or is its 'P' heard; now I'm starting to squirm.
The longer I'm in here, the less sense I make,
 If I don't leave here soon, I'll forget how to bake.
No, I'm not really here going insane
 I just keep running off the curb of memory lane.

On Saturday past, I saw a good flick
    It was about a big spider who killed—how sick!
The name of it was 'Arachnophobia', and
    I jumped in my seat more than I could stand.
Have you seen this movie, it mixes horror with fun
    By the end of the movie, your heart's on the run.
I've always liked spiders until I saw this
    Now spiders are something I know I won't miss.
How is your back, is it hurting you still
    Since you fell at your job and you felt sort of ill?
I hope it is better, and you're short on the pain
    Does it hurt you much more when outside it does rain?
I just can't believe all the rain that we've had
    I guess that the snow pack is not all that bad.
I'm glad at least something is going good for this year
    It can only get better; someday I'll be near.
Earlier today, I had a headache come on.
    But after my shower, the pain was all gone.
I still have the right to shower every day
    But because of the bother, I tell the guard 'Nay.'
I don't work out too much, so I don't really sweat
    And there isn't a reason good enough to get wet.
I still do my push-ups and sit-ups as planned
    But not everyday—just when I've time on my hand.
I rarely go outside since I work all week long
    My spare time is filled up with poems and song.
I hope that this letter has been fun for your eyes
    Please know that I love you, with you my heart lies.
So now I will end all these rhymes I have made
    And I thank you for paying my bills you have paid.
Don't know how I'll do it, but I will pay you back,
    I've got to go now though; time for the sack!

Day 85: April 2, 1991

I saw the counselor assigned to me to discuss my personal views on the case that put me in jail, and to administer more testing that would be used by the judge to decide the sentence I should receive. The conversation was less than pleasing.

The counselor told me some of the things I should expect in the months ahead. She said my case was interesting, and the case was full of holes that my defense attorney should have picked up on. The use of amphetamines by Bob, the knife found at the hospital, the numerous assaults on me previous to the night of my arrest, and the simple fact that it happened at my house were all evidence that I was not the initiator of our confrontation.

Her main conclusion on my case was that I was in jail because of my immoral actions; I was sleeping with someone's wife. What a crock of shit. Excuse me, but I was really pissed off when she told me that. I had a right to be protected from that maniac. My involvement with Mindy did not give him the right to stalk me and try to kill me. (I should point out that the stalking law in California was passed and went into effect on January 1, 1991, too late to be used in my protection.)

What was the law, anyway? Did it only apply to those that the police and judge wanted to apply it to? I felt that I had been treated unfairly by the judge in my case, and I hoped the appeals lawyer could talk some sense into him. (I had no idea how the appeals process worked; and I had no idea that this lawyer was after nothing but money.) Nothing gives one man the right to stalk another man. Nothing. And for me, being locked up was a clear sign that it had been decided that I gave Bob that right. Unbelievable.

We talked about the whole case, and she let me tell my side of the tale. She was very proper, and she gave me some hints to build up my case for sentencing. She said to make sure that the officer in charge of the office wrote me a letter, called a 'chromo', which was like a letter of reference for the work I had performed as a clerk in the office.

She also told me that the psych report from Dr. L. was not in my file. Why it wasn't in my file by that time was a mystery. She said that report would be very crucial in helping the judge make his decision. I told her the judge hated me, and she didn't say anything about that.

She encouraged me to stay out of any trouble, which of course is something I would do regardless of the uprising circumstances. I felt so frustrated about all of this.

I didn't understand how any of the inmates here could be so adjusted to prison life. It didn't make any sense. They lived out the routine from day to day, and the only thing that concerned them was the day they would go to the next prison where they would do the remainder of their time. For most of them, their release date was over a year away, and they didn't care when that was, because they would only be out for a month or two. 65% of those that I met, and I think I am repeating myself, were repeat offenders.

Could our society, as we know it, get better when all that we do is provide free housing for these people? And the law was so concerned with the rights for these people. What about those these people have hurt? Don't they have any rights?

It was clear to me, from these institution walls, how corrupt and inferior the Department of Corrections, at least in California, really was.

The life there was a luxury. Only the inmate who wanted to work did so. All of the inmates who had no such desire were allowed to go outside in the sunshine, play softball, work out with an elaborate weight set, play handball, jog around the 1/4 mile field, play basketball, horseshoes, soccer, and volleyball, socialize with whomever they chose, and relax. No incentive to do anything but enjoy prison was given to the inmates. Only the select few, who couldn't survive like that, would ever have a reason to stay out of the system. I am glad I was one of those few.

My cellmate told me how he used to try to fit in with the 'in' crowd, but never did. Now, he is glad that he didn't fit in. I could relate to that! We got along well enough, and he seemed to be an intelligent guy.

Day 88: April 5, 1991

I was now on my 50th day here at Inacia City. Another 29 to 39 days and I would be on my way home to the county. During the next week, I expected to see the psychiatrist from the prison who would tell me how the testing I took came out. That would be interesting.

The next couple of days were sunny, and being the weekend, I shrugged off my fear of the yard and went outside for 2 hours. It was warm enough for early April that I took off my shirt, and received a slight sunburn for it. It wasn't enough to even notice pain-wise, but the color was a light shade of pink. I put my shirt back on after about an hour to avoid any real exposure. I could see myself trying to be comfy in my cell with a sunburn!

I took a few days off from reading, and I started on my second novel by another well-known writer. He was alright, except he was a little loose with spelling. I picked novels apart! One novel used the word 'lighted' 3 or 4 times. I was appalled to say the least. "I lighted a cigarette," is not correct English, regardless of what a writer is trying to convey.

I was playing more games of 'Casino' solitaire, and I had finally won some games. I must have played 50 games before I won one.

Day 91: April 8, 1991

As of today, I hadn't seen the psychologist with the results of what the psych report (done there) indicated. I hoped it would happen soon.

Not a lot had been happening there. My job in the office, and my clerical skills, had earned me substantial recognition from three of the officers I worked for. (And those were the ones that had mentioned their thoughts on my conviction to me. It was their opinions that I made a big mistake in not hiring a private attorney to represent me. How many others felt that way, I wondered?)

Looking for new ways to take up my time, I was making a picture of some buildings in a city, sort of a high-rise landscape. I'd send the finished product home to my parents when I was done. I figured that it would take me another 6 or 7 days to complete, since I was doing it in the office, and I had to set it aside when work needed to be done. I wasn't jeopardizing my job. The artwork was just a pleasant way to pass the dull hours between 12 & 2 in the afternoon, when not much is happening, and the guards were on their lunch breaks.

Today an officer gave me some ice, a commodity not enjoyed too often inside those walls, so I grabbed a couple of sodas out of my cell, and I must tell you, I enjoyed that ice-cold Dr. Pepper so much! A hot Dr. Pepper, which was the way I had to drink them since I got them last month, was not very tasty. Actually, it was awful!

I had received a letter from my parent's with Mindy's PO box, and since receiving that little bit of information, everything had been wonderful. For example, I had received the letter right before activity time, where we were allowed to congregate in the dining hall to play cards and BS and watch TV. My partner & I were playing spades and were losing all the way up to the last hand. On the last hand, however, we pulled off a big skunk and won the game! Some times, the Lord showed himself in small ways. Interesting how I felt all my good fortunes were related to the letter with Mindy's contact information.

Day 92: April 9, 1991

After receiving the information necessary to write to Mindy again, the warning that such correspondence may lead to a harsher sentence had left me, and I wanted Mindy to know how I was doing.

The thought of holding her close again gave me strength that I needed to get by. Memories of her smile brought me up when I was down. I imagined her voice, and my ears rang with the joy of a thousand blue birds. Despite the knowledge of my return to the county jail to await sentencing, all that I could think about was how much I missed her.

At that point in my life, I felt that I had been such a fool to think that she and I were not right for each other. For so long, I'd let others tell me that she was just playing me, leading me on, and not really the person

I thought she was. I didn't know what her feelings were, and I guess I hoped that she still cared for me. I knew all that had happened in the past was due to her love for me, and I hoped that she still felt the same. If she didn't, I'd understand. I decided that until I heard from her otherwise, I would take for granted that she was still my Special Love.

I had done very well at Inacia City so far. The reception center was not as hardcore as I thought it would be. Instead, I had found many areas that needed to be improved. The criminal system was absolutely putrid. Most of those guys wanted to be there, because this is where all their "Home-Boys" were. They were so weak in mind and character that they couldn't face trying to make it on their own in the free world. What a bunch of losers.

Day 95: April 12, 1991

Corresponding with Mindy directly again made me focus on what might occur after my release. I wanted to get out of Valley City when I was back in the free world. I had always wanted to move up to Alaska for a year or so. Maybe now was the time to do that.

Day 122: May 9, 1991

Most of the letters I wrote for the immediate weeks after getting Mindy's contact information were mindless ramblings from a lonely man to a beautiful woman. I repeated myself constantly in those letters, all of them typed up neatly while I had extra time in the office where I worked. The words "I love you" were written too many times to count, and I can only imagine that Mindy had started to regret allowing me to write to her again!

Working in the office took up time that made the days spent at Inacia City go by practically unnoticed. In my solitude, I found that I felt a future existed for Mindy and I, regardless of the circumstances that had brought us together. I decided to write letters to Mindy that explained my beliefs, my emotions, and my lifestyle so she could be sure that I was the right guy for her.

In those letters, I told her that I was a man brought up in a Christian family with a hardworking father constantly involved in the activities of his children, and a stay-at-home mother who made sure that education and religion came first. I was born into circumstances that many children born in 1963 could only hope for.

I talked about my life growing up in a home where there was never any domestic violence. My father's occupation gave us a modest household, definitely not rich, but not wanting for anything necessary. We never went hungry, and we had a vacation every year without a miss. Our family was full of love that was evident anytime something occurred in our lives. My parents took in 61 foster children, mostly infants, while my brother, sister, and I grew up, holding them for a time until an adoptive family was found.

Day 124: May 11, 1991

I continued to be amazed at how different the system was from what I expected of it. In no way did it fit in with my idea of "locking up a prisoner."

Instead, it seemed to give unearned privileges to the inmates. I didn't know what other state prisons were like, but I was disturbed at what I'd seen since I began my incarceration.

Here at the Northern California Medical Facility in Inacia City, CA, the prisoners were allowed to get out of their cells for any reason that they could present to the officer of their wing or "tier" in a 'It's really true' manner.

All day long, from the time breakfast was finished being served, the halls were crowded with inmates who had no reason to be out of their cells. They constantly walked around and teased the inmates that were locked up in their cell in a playful manner.

But this was not prison to them. It was their home. They were not expected to pay for their room and board, their food, or their clothing. They were allowed to go to a store (canteen) once a month and buy up to seventy dollars worth of food, toiletries, and other miscellaneous items, mainly tobacco.

I, for one, objected to being pinned in a cell with fifty other inmates who were busy killing themselves and every one else around them with their filthy tobacco smoke. It was 1991, and the law prohibiting smoking in state offices was enforced in every other place that I knew of, but not there. Why, I wondered?

Day 128: May 15, 1991

This was my 90th day at Inacia City, and I jumped at every sound that remotely sounded like my name and the instructions to pack my things and get ready to return to Valley City for my sentencing hearing. I had not learned what the results of either the state psychiatrist's, nor the privately hired psychiatrist's, reports had suggested in my behalf.

Now, each day went by more slowly than the day before.

Not known at the time, I would be at Inacia City for another 15 days before I received word that I was to return to Valley City for my sentencing.

Day 129: May 16, 1991

I had come to the conclusion by this time that the officials running the prisons in California figured that inmates had a right to infringe on the free air rights of others. It was an example of the blatant teaching to convicts that they, the convicts, were special, and did not have to obey the law; they could do as they pleased.

While I was in the county Ranch, I remember hearing one inmate give his feelings on this matter. "Yea, they cut smoking from the county jails," he said, "but they won't do it in the prison system. Then they'd have a riot on their hands. The convicts would take over if they tried to enforce that."

Was this guy right? Were the officials of California afraid to take away the cigarettes and chew that the inmates regarded as essential to their existence?

In there, you could get artwork, food, clothes, favors from other inmates, and who knows what else if you have tobacco to trade. Most inmates had a can of tobacco, but if you could get a pack of Malboros, you would then be seen as an upper tier inmate.

I comically thought that it may be that the officials wanted the prisoners to continue smoking so that they would get cancer and die, and then they are out of the system in a shorter period of time than would have necessarily occurred had the inmate not had access to tobacco.

I had to take up smoking for a while, at two to four cigarettes a day, just to cope with the haze that hung in the air of my cell. I had smoked a little bit before my incarceration, but when I smoked before, it was never an inconvenience to anyone around me. I always checked to see if anyone minded the smoke. If there were an affirmative answer, I wouldn't smoke. It was that simple. Here, one doesn't dare say that he is "offended by the smoke." It could mean violence, which is just about all that the inmates talk about.

Day 132: May 19, 1991

Sometimes the thought patterns of the inmates was pretty clear by the statements they made. "The only good cop is a dead cop." I'd heard it so many times while I was locked up.

They also freely verbalized their thoughts on how to treat a woman. When watching a television show in the dorm, if a woman was sticking up for herself, the convicts would all scream in harmony, "Slap the bitch! If that was my woman I'd knock the shit out of her." And I'm sure that they mean it, too.

As strange as is seemed to me, the inmates loved to watch the cop shows, like "DEA", "Most Wanted", "Cops", and all the rest of the shows that depicted reenactments of violence that had been committed against innocent victims. And they really enjoyed it. They would sit there very quietly and discuss ways that they would improve on the scheme when they were released so they could get away with the crime. When someone would get beat up, whether the good guy or the bad guy (at least they weren't picky about who got it, as long as someone did), they'd all applaud at what I found to be revolting. The sympathetic programs were rarely watched because every one of the inmates was so busy being macho that they couldn't afford to let their feelings be brought to the surface.

One good thing in those men that I discovered was their total denunciation of rape. Anyone who was convicted of rape had best not let the general population find out about that, or he'd be dead at the earliest convenient time.

I didn't get it. How was it wrong to rape a woman, but okay to slap her around?

Day 134: May 21, 1991

Let me describe the yard and the allowed outside activities. The inmates here were allowed out on the yard from nine to two every day. They had access to the yard area which for this place was a six acre spread, outfitted with a baseball field, a soccer field, a couple of basketball courts, four horseshoe pits, a handball court, and an elaborate weight pile. A yard shack was in the corner of the yard to give out the necessary equipment for the various sports, since the bats and gloves and balls must be assigned to an inmate. This was done by trading the inmate's ID card for the equipment requested. Although an officer sits in the shack, it was actually run by other inmates. I had a problem with the yard scene.

Why was it that convicts were allowed out of their cells at all? I had been paying taxes for eight years, and I didn't think it was right that taxes pay for guards to sit and watch convicts play in the sun. I expected to sit in a cell for the entire stay here. Instead, I found a virtual amusement park. And that's what it was called.

"I'd rather do two years here than one year in the county," I'd overheard countless inmates say since my arrival. It was too easy for these outcasts of society. No wonder they wanted to come back. And this place, the reception center in Inacia City State Prison, was the toughest to get through. After an inmate was processed, he would go on to another facility that was even more lax than this one. I didn't doubt it. I constantly told about "the right of the convict."

The most popular form handed out from the office was a 602 form: Inmate Appeals Form. This form was a formal complaint that an inmate filled out against someone of the institution. The inmates would collaborate stories so that the officer in question is made to look suspicious when he denies the accusations that ten inmates had all claimed he was guilty of. I saw it take place one night.

An inmate threw food on another inmate in play in the mess hall. When the officer in charge took action against the guilty inmate, the other inmates, his buddies, all banded together with a 602 form in each individual's hand, to denounce the officer's actions. They all claimed that it wasn't the convict in question.

Of course, you know and I know that the officer was doing exactly as he should have. But in there, the inmates had come to expect a bit of leniency towards their actions. No matter how loud they'd get, they expected the officer to look the other way. I didn't think it should be like that.

To make it worse, it appeared that the guards grew more lenient as their years of service progressed. The older guards took all kinds of back talk from inmates, excuses for being where they shouldn't be, and reasons that they should be let out of their cells.

The guards had a form they were required to fill out when an inmate or group of inmates got out of hand, called a CDC-115, a disciplinary report. The paper work involved in writing one of these forms was so lengthy that the guards usually didn't have the time to fill it out, and they didn't have the desire to fill it out, either. A 115 was usually met by a 602 from the reported inmate. Then the guard would have to go through the hassle of seeing his Lieutenant, explaining his reason for such actions that were taken, and face a possible disciplinary action against himself. I thought such treatment of the guards was absolutely terrible. These forms made it appear that the inmate had more clout than the guard.

Day 138: May 25, 1991

While working in the office at the Inacia City Reception Center, I was stunned to find a folder that pertained to financial aide available to ex-convicts. The following is a listing of financial aid available from the Social Security Administration office for paroled convicts.

Applications for these funds could be requested from a prisoner's parole officer.

FEDERAL ASSISTANCE:
Employment Insurance @ $27 to $52 per week.
Social Security Insurance of $325.00 per month.
Social Security Payments of $225.00 per week.
Food Stamps totaling $80.00 per week.
SBA (Federal) loans up to $50,000.00.
Pel Grants up to $3,000.00 per term.
Cal Grants up to $1,500.00 per term.

STATE ASSISTANCE:
Will pay up to two weeks in a motel after release.
Will help you get on General Assistance (Welfare).
Will give you up to $250.00 for clothing.
Will assist you in getting government loans with low interest up to $15,000.
Will pay your first and last months rent.
Will assist you in deposits on phone, gas and other utilities.
Will give you a bus pass.
Will give you enough money to live on for two weeks.
Will pay you to go to school.
Will help you find a job.

DISADVANTAGED MINORITIES:

Vietnam Veterans, Ex-Felons, per federal law (the Economic Act of 1975), repeals the moral interpretude clause. As a convicted felon, your rights have been restored to the extent that you are now able to obtain any license necessary for any business you may need, i.e. liquor, real estate, insurance broker, contractor's license, etc. However, this is only true if your conviction was not related to your prospective type of business.

BONDING:

You are bondable through the employment office and the bond can be obtained through your parole office, with a $10,000 limit. It is the law!

REBOUND:

A program staffed with ex-felons that operates through the department of sociology, to help ex-felons reenter society through a college based program. They will help you get admitted to any college in the state and they will assist you in obtaining grants and loans.

CURRENT LEGISLATION (1991):

Provides that you do not have to pay back grants for the following uses:
$1,900 for a car;
$400 for tools;
$300 for work clothes;
$400 for dress clothes;
The maximum amount is $3,000.00, and this is available through your parole office.

SMALL BUSINESS ADMINISTRATION:

SBA loans can be obtained through a DVR (Department of Vocation al Rehabilitation) counsel or direct application. SBA can guarantee a loan up to $250,000.00. They will also help you put this loan to good use, through an organization called "Score."

As I typed all of that information, I realized that any one who can't make it on the outside with all of this free aide must be a serious loser.

"Oh yeah," I thought, "most of them are!"

Day 143: May 30, 1991

I completed my 90 day observation period and was returned to the Ranch near Valley City.

Day 147: June 3, 1991

I was only at the Ranch for a few days before being taken downtown to the city jail where I would be held until my sentencing hearing. When that day would come, I did not know.

However, the time went by quickly, as I now had access to a telephone, daily, which I would use to call Mindy and speak to her directly. The sound of her voice was exciting!

It would be 12 days before the sentencing hearing.

Day 158: June 14, 1991

When the day for the sentencing hearing finally arrived, I was quite surprised at what occurred. Of course, I had been hoping for a sentence of probation with time served. The 90 day observation reports had come back to the judge with recommendations for probation. The personal psychiatrist, Dr. L., recommended probation. The probation officer assigned to my case even recommended probation.

But the judge said no to probation. My heart sank. Here it comes. Hard time. Years of my life were going to be wasted, sitting in a cell with a pile of puke that wanted to be locked up because it was easy.

Damn.

And then the words that followed out of the judge's mouth were even more surprising!

"I'll stay the use of the knife as a deadly weapon, and sentence the defendant to 18 months in state prison," he read calmly as I sat awestruck.

The use of a knife as a deadly weapon carried a mandatory 3 years in prison. No exceptions. And the judge threw that out.

How could he throw out the main piece of evidence in the case? Unless he saw through the D.A.'s game and knew that the knife found at the hospital should have been checked for prints at the time and wasn't.

With an 18 month sentence, and getting halftime for good behavior, I would be home—at least I could—be home by Christmas time. I stood and turned to my family and friends behind me as the bailiff once again put the cuffs on me.

I made eye contact with my friend, Tony, and in an instant we both knew that I had just gotten extremely lucky. It wasn't until I arrived back at Inacia City State Prison that I learned exactly how much the judge had really helped me.

As it turned out, if you are convicted of a crime and sentenced to probation, then you must pay all of the fines and levies placed on you by the judge. You are considered able to pay them. However, if you are convicted of a crime and are given a prison sentence, then the state pays the fine for you, and you have no fines or levies to pay when you leave the walls of imprisonment.

The fines levied against me were about $12,000.00. And because the judge gave me a short prison sentence instead of a jail sentence, I didn't have to pay a dime of it. Was this the reason the judge gave me prison time? I would come to believe that it was as the days ahead went by.

Day 169: June 25, 1991

A few days in the city jail, then a week at the Ranch, and then I would be back in Inacia City, where I would learn of which prison I would spend the remainder of my sentence at.

On the morning of my return to Inacia City, it was chaotic from the start.

The day started at 2am that morning for me. The guards decided that they wanted to do a surprise inspection so they made everyone get up and go to the showers from each cell while they searched the cell quite thoroughly.

The inmates who smoked (and cigarettes weren't allowed on RBF) were always getting cigs smuggled in. But with no matches, they had to arc the plug on the TV, and make the spark light a piece of tissue. Well, after years of doing this, the metal part of the plug broke off! So, while searching that morning, they noticed that the plug was broken, and took it away for repairs. They said it would be back in 24 hours. I wasn't going to hold my breath. So, after about a half hour and losing our TV, we were returned to our cell.

At 5:30am, they served us breakfast as usual. The food was bad—biscuits covered with watery gravy, oatmeal, an orange, and 2 pieces of wheat bread (and a pint of LF milk). So, the day was continuing to be screwed up.

After breakfast, they start calling names. That was how they called me the first time I was to leave here. Well, names were called, but mine never was! So I figured I wasn't going anywhere, and I went back to sleep. At 7am, I was awakened to hear my name! I was leaving that shit-hole after all!

The rest of the morning went the same as it had during my previous transfer to Inacia City. 26 people were piled into a holding cell for about 1½ hours. Then we stripped off the orange clothes and were given our street clothes for the ride to Inacia City. Of course, all that I had were the green clothes I wore here (at Vac) before, so I was easy to notice as a returnee.

After getting dressed, they decided to cuff me separately, not with the chain gang! Then, I got the front seat on the bus! Too cool! I didn't have to sit with all the smelly inmates who don't shower back in the back!

The trip was OK. But I noticed something very different as the bus approached the hills. They were all brown! When I had left for my sentencing hearing those hills were so beautiful that I was constantly reminded of Mindy when I looked at them. What a difference 2 months can make!

Being back at Inacia City was worse than I remembered it. I didn't have a job, and I didn't know anyone. All of the inmates I had come to know previously had moved on to the next prison where they would serve out the remainder of their sentences.

They had made a number of changes since I'd left there almost 2 months before. The time for activity time in the mess hall had changed from 5:30pm to 8pm now instead of 7:30pm to 9pm as it had been previously. The times on the yard had been altered. So I felt out of place in a place I wanted no part of.

All of the officers had forgotten me also. Guess I just didn't have that home-boy look to me, like so many others that they did remember. Of course, the fact that they kept coming back year after year may have had something to do with that too. So I just laid there in my cell, and slept and wrote and stared out of the window towards Valley City and thought about Mindy.

I was hoping to be sent to the old Appalsha Prison "Camp", a place that held low risk inmates. That would have been close to Mindy, and I'd been told it wasn't too bad as far as prisons were. And there I was, believing what the inmates were telling me, despite the number of times that I had found their opinions to be opposite of what I considered acceptable.

I had a cellmate that didn't talk much, and was a repeat offender. We didn't have much in common, so our conversations were short and infrequent. He was in for petty theft. I hoped to move on to the next prison quickly.

Day 170: June 26, 1991

Only back for 1 day, I was able to secure another job as a janitor in the counselors' office. While I worked there, I was able to speed up the process of getting in to see my counselor. Once I was able to see him, he'd be able to tell me how much time I had left of my sentence, and where I would be serving that time. I found out that there was a level 1 Camp there at Inacia City, but if I could get into "Old Appalsha Camp", that was my first choice.

My job was very laidback. I worked for about 15 minutes, then sat and socialized with other inmates for about an hour. Then another 15 minutes of work, and another hour on the butt. That was the way convicts worked. The fact that I'd only been back at Inacia City for 2 days, and I already had a job, made this 'stay' seem to be off to a good start! The hours were formidable—I'd arrive at my work site at 7:30am after breakfast and stay until 3pm. Then I'd go back to my cell for dinner and count, and then return to the work site until 8:30pm. I was practically never in my cell. With any luck, I'd be out of Inacia City before too long, as well.

Again, I had the benefit of access to pen and paper. I had always had access to writing material since I started serving time in prison.

I was also in a position that would allow me to find out sooner-than-normal if any of my family or Mindy had been approved for a visit. Having this job was practically a dream come true; it made a bad situation a little bit better.

My cellmate was getting easier to talk with as we got to know each other. He wasn't the type of guy I'd hang around with on the streets. He was into the drug scene, and he was that macho type of guy that women just love . . . where's the toilet, I'm gonna puke! Yea, he was that type of male chauvinist. The kind of guy I just didn't relate to. And most of the people there were just like him, so he was "at home". I couldn't wait to get the hell out of there!

The weather was crazy that summer. I was pleasantly surprised that it wasn't hotter than hell, the norm for that time of year. I would have been dying if it had been. But the cool weather was just another part of my incarceration that had gone my way, so to speak. I hoped the rest of my time would go as well.

Day 171: June 27, 1991

It was nice having a job in the counselors' office. The inmates were allowed to drink real coffee while working there. It was freshly made with a coffee machine (10 cup) and, lo & behold, it was Folgers! MMM. Mountain Grown! I drank so much coffee on my first day that I couldn't sleep.

I took my first shower in three days tonight after I returned from work around 8:30pm (thank God for deodorant). I had to wash my hair with bar soap. I didn't have any shampoo yet because I hadn't been to canteen yet, which wasn't open until after the 4th of July weekend. A real advantage to working so late was that I was able to take a shower every night, for as long as I wanted, without a 3 minute time limit as the other prisoners had. And I was able to take my shower alone, so I didn't have to worry if I dropped the soap.

I had to revert back to using a pencil because the officer on my floor took my pen. Apparently, I was not supposed to have one like that. He had come to my cell to give me my ID card, but since I was at work at the counselors' office, he kept it with him. He was off for the weekend, so I had to wait until that following Monday before I could get it.

Day 173: June 29, 1991

It was Saturday now, and I didn't know if I wanted to go out to the yard or go to work. There was a bullshit punk that also worked there, with the impression in his own mind that he was God's gift, like most punks. He was supposed to leave yesterday, but didn't. And he had begun to get on my nerves. He always had some type of bullshit to say, something I had termed "typical convictitis".

I eventually did decide to go outside, for the first time since I'd returned to Inacia City. I did a couple of sets of curls and overhead lifts, and walked around the yard a couple of times. I was only out there from 12 to 1pm because after going out to the yard, I had decided not to stay.

You see, they would call "Yard out" (time to go outside) at 12 noon, and call "Yard in" by each wing starting at about 12:30pm. By the time they started calling "Yard In" to my wing, it was 1pm and I'd had enough of the sun.

I went straight back to work from the yard and never even saw my cell. When I came back from work, they had already started dinner so I just got into line. After eating dinner, I returned to my cell, and I was feeling the workout, a little sore.

I found out that without an ID card, I couldn't go to the gym at night for activities. This was just another of the many things changed since I was here last time. It used to be that those inmates that wanted could go to the dining hall every other night from 7:30 until 9:00, to play cards, drink coffee, or just shoot the shit. Well, now the routine was to go every night to the gym, where one could lift weights, play basketball, or play cards and shoot the shit. Of course, you had to have an ID card. Which eliminated me, because I didn't get my ID card back when the guard came to give it to me, and I wasn't in my cell.

While at work on Friday, the old man who was the head of inmates called me over to him and gave me a pass to the lab. Then he said to me,

"Gee, Gordan, I'm awful sorry but your AIDS test came back positive. They want you to go down and give some more blood so they can retest you."

Well, he didn't fool me. I had only given blood on Thursday, and I knew that the test took at least two weeks to come back. As it turned out, it was all a joke. Sort of an initiation as a worker there. He was asking me questions like, "Are you gay?" and "You ever slam (shoot-up) dope?" and "Do you eat pussy?" I answered with two 'Nos' and a yes, respectively.

Apparently, they pulled the same gag on everybody who worked there. One guy broke down and confessed to fucking a couple of street whores after a fight with his old lady. Another was found tying

63

a noose to hang himself with! Still another started crying and said, "I can't tell my girlfriend!" and they said, "But if you don't, she'll just spread it to others." He cried harder! Pretty cruel, eh? That's prison for you. How exciting! What else could we do for fun?

I took advantage of my work pass tonight. I stopped the guard as he walked by and asked him if I could take shower. The wing still took only one side of the wing per night, and my side was tomorrow night. I showed him my work pass, and he opened the door; no questions!

I still had to wash my hair with bar soap, but my hair was starting to look pretty greasy. My blond hair showed the dirt and oil a lot more than darker hair.

Later that night, my cellmate showed me a couple of porno books he was able to get. Imagine that; inside a state prison, inmates were able to sneak in pornographic material. What else can they get in?

Day 174: June 30, 1991

Today I witnessed another event that I couldn't write about. Instead, I had to recall the details of the events as they unfolded. The man who I had seen get knocked to the ground by a sucker-punch was out of the infirmary and back in with the general population. According to my cellmate, his jaw had been broken, and the back of his head required a number of stitches where it had hit the hardball court. My cellmate had told me that the brothers (whites) had learned who the sucker-puncher was and that the brothers would take care of this punk in their own style.

Then the day became interesting. All of the inmates were required to go out to the field. A thorough search of the cells was going to be done, a 'shake down', as it's called in prison. So I was forced back out on to the yard where I really didn't like to go.

I was talking with my cellmate when suddenly one of his friends approached. My cellmate told me to, "Stay here," and walked away. I watched him as he walked through the crowd of prisoners. Then I saw him, the punk inmate who had sucker punched the other on the handball court in the months before.

From where I was, I could see that 7 or 8 other inmates, which I knew as 'homeys' of my cellmate, were approaching the punk from different sides.

Without warning, a shank appeared in one of the inmate's hands. About four inches long, it had been fashioned out of some type of metal from who knows where.

The punk took it in the stomach, and then the inmate shuffle occurred. This is where about 30 inmates all bunch up around the attack and all make passing movements as if passing the weapon off to the next. This way no one knows who ends up with the shank, and it's available for the next time some inmate needed to be shanked.

I'd say that word of this retribution attack had been leaked to the guards, hence the reason we were all out on the yard and all of the cells were being searched.

The punk never even complained to the guards that he had a 4 inch deep gash in his side. He apparently sought first aid only after leaving the yard that day. I was amazed that none of the guards saw him bleeding through his shirt on the way back into the housing unit.

And that's the way inmates administer punishment. The punk did show his true colors by not going to the guards. He most likely knew that this retaliation was coming, and he took it like a man.

Day 175: July 1, 1991

It had finally warmed up. After all the cool weather, it was a shocker, but it was finally feeling like summer time! It was nice, working in the counseling center all day. It was air-conditioned. Let me emphasize that . . . AIR—CONDITIONED!

Yes, it was very nice to be so privileged to work in an air-conditioned office. I enjoyed it! At work, I was given "stamp detail". I had to stamp 400 passes with three different stamps. Each stamp went in a particular spot on the pass, and the need to be exact made the time go by very fast, as it required a good amount of concentration.

I didn't seem to be gaining any weight, and I wasn't eating lunch at all. I had become use to it by now, so I was only hungry about an hour before dinner. They would serve the box lunches with that 'mystery meat' in it, and I didn't take to it very well.

Surprisingly, my cell was not too hot in the short amounts of time that I was in it. I hoped it would remain that way. I'm sure it could be very uncomfortable if it didn't.

Day 176: July 2, 1991

Today was shitty. I received my new clothes at clothing exchange, which occurs weekly. I turned in my sheets and dirty clothes for clean sheets and clothes. I was at work, so I took a little break (I had my clothes with me since morning), and went to do the exchange. Of course, when I returned to my cell I remembered to bring my clean clothes from work with me, right?

NO! I left them at the job sight! Now I'm going to have to sleep on the mattress with no sheets! Ugh! It was hot in the cell, so I didn't have the need to cover up with anything. But leaving the laundry in the counselors' office made me feel so stupid.

That incident made me reflect on the many times I was so dumb in the past. I was educated and intelligent, I thought, but I did my share of asinine shit. I wonder if my mom was right? She thought that I had some type of lingering brain damage from the motorcycle accident (in February, 1983) that led to the incident that brought me here. At the time, I thought she was just making excuses for my stupidity. Unfortunately, I'd find out in 16 years that she was correct.

I hadn't received any mail from my family for a while. It was interesting how the best part of the day was when the officer dropped a letter under the cell door! Everybody there felt that way.

Day 177: July 3, 1991

Hot! The word of the day was hot. HOT! "F" me. I sat in the counseling center all day, then went back to my cell, that shithole of an oven! Ouch!

I waited to take a shower after getting back to my cell. It seemed to have cooled off about 5 degrees in the short time I was there. I was told at work today that 5 inmates had died in the last 24 hours from heat-related causes. I had to wonder if there was any truth to that.

I finally received the reports from the probation office, the psychiatrist who saw me (Dr. L.), my dump-truck public defender, and from the testing and the psychiatrist there at Inacia City. As I read them, I couldn't understand what I was doing there. I just wanted to die. Right then, I didn't really care. I felt like my life was screwed up beyond repair. I looked at all the stupid shit inmates, and I wondered how the hell did I ever get there? What a rotten place it was.

A man entered our cell and took the temperature. It was only 94 degrees F in the cell. Odd, I thought it was cooler than that. He said it was 101 outside.

Last night, they served us Mexican food for dinner, and in the 15 minutes I sat in the chow hall, I broke out in a serious sweat. It must have been 110 degrees F in there.

At 2:00 today (July 4), an officer with an attitude, who I've never seen before, came into where I worked and told me to leave, along with the other white worker. He let the punk stay there, of course, because he (the guard) didn't want to be 'prejudice'.

All of the regular guards were gone for the holiday, so this weekend really sucked. The replacement guard who was there for the weekend to relieve the original guards didn't want to have 3 clerks in the office, so he sent me and one of the other inmates back to our cells. This led to some bitter feelings, because the one clerk he kept was the punk that I had so many problems with.

The letters I'd been writing to Mindy and family relayed all of the bad thoughts and feelings I'd been experiencing over the last few days, but I was actually doing fine. I wrote down my feelings so I could remember them. I thought it would be important to remember those emotions when my incarceration was over and done.

They fed us pork chops for dinner—big, fat, juicy ones. They were actually good! One of the best meals I'd had since I'd been locked up.

Mindy had started a new job, so my thoughts were with her, hoping it would work out. I knew how some jobs start off great and then wither into a mundane, "Do I have to go to work again?" job.

I knew I wouldn't be going back to my job until Monday. I didn't like being chosen to leave instead of a punk. I hated punks more than ever, now! The scum in prison, and the way they talked, was enough to make me puke 10 times! And considering my profession, that's pretty bad!

Day 179: July 5, 1991

A new day, and so far, it had been going pretty well. When I arrived at work that morning, Tom had come over and dropped off about 10 novels. That helped fill in the time! With the books and the job, I remember having little time to be bored.

I did a little work (cleaned the windows) and then played cards and typed a letter to my mother. I hadn't heard from my parents in a couple of weeks, so with little else to do, I was beginning to worry that something was wrong.

It was pleasant when I arrived back to my cell from work. A nice sea breeze was keeping the temperature down there.

I learned I was incorrect about the weekend schedule. Apparently, it was a regular day. I thought we'd be on a vacation day schedule, but not so. I was allowed to return to work after count until 8:30. And then I finally got to take a shower. Once again, I hadn't had one in 3 days! Yes, I'd been taking a sponge bath, but that wasn't the same. What really got to me was learning that the other wing was getting 3 showers a day to deal with the heat!

Day 180: July 6, 1991

It was another nice day, with a sea breeze keeping the temperature down. After doing only a slight bit of work in the morning, I decided to take the rest of the day off. I was sleepy because I read a book I started on last night until about 11:00pm. It was about a Russian hijacking of a U.S. Space shuttle! I read 150 pages last night.

Day 181: July 7, 1991

It was Sunday, and I had just returned from work and dinner. We had "shake & bake" chicken that was pretty good. I worked really hard today. I don't know why, I just got busy, and kept on going. I planned to go out to the yard tonight and get some exercise. The weather was very nice on the yard at night, when the sea breeze comes in.

Day 184: July 10, 1991

As rare as they were, every now and then I had what amounted to a "good" day.

The day started off wrong. I froze last night! It was really cold, and I couldn't get the damn window to shut. After cuddling up in a ball, the sun finally came up, and since the morning sun shines in the cell, it warms up quickly.

But then things changed for me. After I had gotten up and dressed for breakfast and work, respectively, I started fooling with the window to see why it wouldn't close. Much to my pleasure, I found that all that was necessary to close the dumb thing was to pull up on the bottom. I guessed it was getting jammed on something somewhere.

And breakfast was actually good!

I arrived at work after chow, and the punk that I'd had a problem with was sent away, to another prison. He never did anything the entire time I was there. Typical. As a matter of fact, the boss had told him to mop the floors on Monday night before he left. Well, that lazy piece of shit didn't do it. He just sat there all night and talked with the black officer and the other black inmate (a blue shirt). When I arrived to work Tuesday (yesterday) morning, the boss said, "Go home, take the day off." I had to go to the yard because that shit-head didn't do what he was told to. Well, I mean I didn't get to work. I went to the yard at 12 noon and came back in at 2pm, and wow, I noticed that I had been sunburned.

The new green shirt hired to replace the punk at my job was cool and easy to get along with, so another plus.

Today was canteen day, and I spent $30.00 on personal items, including shampoo, soup and a soapdish, thongs, toothpaste, dental floss, Q-tips, cards, fingernail clippers, a mug, a 6 pack of cherry RC Cola, some aloe vera lotion, 1 can of Buglar tobacco, and 3 packs of cigarettes. The best thing about canteen was I was first in line. Ha! I didn't have to wait for anybody! I wished it was always like that.

After that, I saw my counselor! I was informed that I'd be going to the Appalsha Ranch or Stony Brook near Ione, and I was eligible for the work furlough program. I had applied for the work furlough and was hoping I'd be able to get a job with the real world!

I had purchased two packs of Camels for the blue shirt who got me in to see my counselor so soon. I'd made a deal with him that if he got me in to see him, I'd get him a couple of packs of cigarettes when I went to canteen. He upheld his part of the bargain, so I did too.

Then tonight, I received a 'tiger' letter (a letter written on paper with tigers in the background) from Mindy. I loved it! I put it in the cell window so I could see it whenever I was in the cell.

So it was an exceptionally good day. The weather remained cool, which was real nice (even if it meant freezing at night!). I had changed my mind on the heat; I no longer preferred the heat over the cold. It was easier to warm up with a blanket than to cool down!

While I was there on the reception side, I wouldn't get any pay or time off for working. I only received the benefit of being out of my cell all day, and the other advantages that went with the job.

Day 185: July 11, 1991

Today, I found 4 gray hairs in my beard. I shaved every 3 to 4 days, and as I was looking in the mirror at work, there they were. I couldn't believe it. Gray hair! I knew I just had to accept it—I wasn't a spring chicken anymore. But I still had a few good clucks left in me.

Well, last night, I started reading a book, and as I started to read the end, I felt that something was wrong. With 50 pages left to read, I couldn't see how the story could end. So I flipped to the end, and son of a bitch, pages were missing! I figure at least 50 were gone. I didn't notice it when I picked it up. Another book got me. I'd lost track of how many books were like that in the prison.

So there I was, only now I was laughing because this was the worst novel I'd ever read. And being that it was a written by a renowned author made it really discouraging. The author was supposed to write such great stuff. This book made two of his books that I hadn't liked. I had read another of his books during my last stay there, and I hadn't liked that one, either. No more of his books for me.

At work I did absolutely nothing! There just wasn't anything to do. I watched T.V., typed up a letter, and played 'spades' with another inmate.

When night came, we had one crappy little dinner, and I do mean crappy and little! It consisted of a piece of meat loaf about 5" x 3" and ½" thick. Then they gave us a hamburger bun to hide it so we wouldn't taste it. And we were given a scoop of cottage cheese (no sugar), pasta salad, and butterscotch pudding. What a treat! Must have been 400 calories in the whole meal. Boy, the budget cuts sure were hitting the CDC, weren't they?

They painted our cell while I was at work on Wednesday. Instead of the green paint with graffiti all over it, it was now a beige color. We couldn't write on the wall or we'd get a 115, a disciplinary mark. Oh, well. It sure was different from all the shit that was in there before. But they (the painters) sure were messy. They put drops of paint everywhere, on the toilet, on the sink, all over the floor, and even on the box springs. When I was a painter last time I was there, we taped up the toilet and sink, and put a cover over the floor. I guess the tape was too expensive for a state that is $14.7 billion in the red!

I continued to smoke cigarettes. I bought a can of Bugle tobacco from the canteen for $5.00 and I would get about 300 cigarettes from it. A hell of a lot cheaper than by the pack, which was almost $2 per pack of 20.

Day 187: July 13, 1991

On Saturday, I went out and played baseball, or rather, softball. I got two hits, but I really played lousy at second base. I dropped a popfly, I missed a throw for a double play, and I fumbled a grounder. It was really windy, that was my excuse, and I was really out of practice. I guessed if I played more I'd be better, but I rarely go out, so I wasn't too concerned about my performance.

Day 190: July 16,1991

When you're locked up, emotions can get the best of you. Your judgment can become impaired, and you even write things down that you don't mean to say. I'd received a letter from Mindy which set me off, and I wrote one of those letters, responding with some words that I regretted.

Her letter explained that she told her kids about our plans to be together, and somehow, in my state of mind, I thought it would actually be possible for her to not tell her children to know about our plans, ever.

I still felt threatened by Mindy's ex-husband, yet he had told the children that he was afraid of me coming after him after I was released. I didn't want that bullshit on my head. Mindy had told her daughter that everything that had happened was because of him. He was a fool, and he had proved it time and time again. He continued to show it by thinking I'd mess up any more of my life just to do something to him.

I was the last person in the world that would do anything to her ex. If something did happen to him, Mindy would have to take back the children. And I'd be out of the picture for good. I also knew that if something did happen to her ex, I'd be the first on the list of suspects with the police.

Day 191: July 17, 1991

Bad news comes when you least expect it.

I received my endorsement on this day, which meant I'd be leaving Inacia City the following week. Although my counselor had told me that I'd be going to the Appalsha Ranch, and the work furlough program, that was not where they decided to send me. That would have been too easy on me and Mindy and everybody else around me.

I was instead being sent to a place down south, right near Bakersfield. It was in the desert somewhere in the middle of nowhere, about 4 hours away from Valley City.

This, of course, meant visits from Mindy were completely out of the question. I was so stunned when I received the endorsement that I felt like throwing up. It took me about 15 minutes just to come to grips with the fact that I was not going to see Mindy for another six months. It seemed that the next time I'd see her was so far away now, when just 30 minutes before I had been talking with the other workers about how soon I would be seeing her.

I was told that the reason I was sent there instead of Appalsha was because I wasn't married. If I had been, the system would have kept me as close to home as possible, but I was judged to be a worthless scumbag since I was single. Another lesson learned.

Day 192: July 18, 1991

Today I had been very busy working at my job. My co-worker and I usually played between three and five games of two-handed spades, which we did just about every day to pass the time. We were on our first game of the day, when the Lieutenant walked into the office, and saw us. He reamed the officer in charge of the office, and he subsequently came down on us, the workers. The Lieutenant told the officer he wanted the stairwell that lead downstairs swept and cleaned to perfection.

Well, I got started and turned the job into a serious project, against the wishes of the other workers. I told them I wasn't going to do a half ass job, so if they didn't want to help, they didn't have to. I liked working alone better anyway. Of course, they took advantage of what I said. Don't get me wrong: they weren't lazy. There was other work to do. So for next two hours, I scrubbed the walls, swept the floor, mopped it, mopped it again, mopped it a third time, and a fourth, and a fifth! Between each mop job, I had to change the water. It was filthy since it hadn't been cleaned in about three years (my estimate!).

After I finished, the officer of the office called the officer in charge of my floor, and asked him if it would be alright if I came back to the wing and took a shower. He okayed it, so I was allowed to freshen myself up. I was filthy! But I sure did feel good at that point in time. And I was pretty worn-out from all the work. I really went overboard. But I always did. I was an extremist.

I was really surprised to receive a letter from Mindy dated July 15th on the 17th. That meant the letter only sat in the mailroom for one day. That was a lot quicker than most letters would arrive. They normally took about a week.

Knowing that work furlough was not going to happen for me had me fighting with depression. I knew that I would be too far away for Mindy for her to come and visit me. She would have to drive for 4 to 4 ½ hours just to get to the prison in Mountaincrest, and then a visit would last maybe two, three hours at the most, and then she would have to drive all the way home again. It just didn't sound feasible. I also worried that her old car would break down somewhere in the middle of the desert on I-5.

The sunburn I experienced wasn't as bad as I first thought. I was able to treat it with some aloe vera lotion, and it didn't hurt that much at all the next day.

Day 193: July 19, 1991

And then desperation set in. After writing to Mindy and discussing the long drive to the new prison I'd be at as too far, I had second thoughts. I really didn't want to try to do the rest of my time without seeing Mindy. Maybe there was a bus route from Sac that she could take down to where I'd be and visit me. I had been thinking about it since I decided I didn't want her driving down to Mountaincrest in her car. Or maybe she could borrow somebody's car that was dependable?

I turned in my property to the office, so that meant the bus taking me down south would leave sometime early Monday morning. I was looking forward to getting out of Inacia City and getting started on my half time at Mountaincrest.

Day 194: July 20, 1991

Today I saw something that absolutely blew my mind. Once again, it was an event that I couldn't write home about. On the eve of the

19th, I was in the dining hall for a game of cards when I noticed two people playing cards together.

It was the punk who sucker-punched the friend of my old cellmate from my previous stay at Inacia City, and the recipient of the broken jaw!

Not only were they playing cards together, they were on the same team! I couldn't believe that two guys, one who'd had his jaw broken and a severe concussion inflicted on him, and the other who'd received a large, potentially fatal knife wound to the gut, could actually be homeys.

It just goes to show, I thought to myself. These people are just plain stupid with no morals. No one in his right mind would forgive the other for the violations that these two had either directly or indirectly committed against the other.

As long as I lived, I'd never forget the end to this story—I could not believe that the two were friends. Hell, it had only been 3 months! That's the intelligence of prisoners, though. None to almost none.

Knowing that I couldn't write about this to home, I did my best to laugh off the event.

I was so glad to have a wonderful woman like Mindy. I had a new cellmate by now, and he hadn't received a letter since he arrived here, and he came in on the bus with me!

I felt bad for the poor guy. Every night he waited for a letter, but nothing ever came. He acted like the tough guy, and didn't say anything, but I know that he was hoping for some mail. Mindy made me feel like a king, getting mail almost every day.

Instead of my being unmarried, I learned that the real reason I was being sent to Mountaincrest was because of a shortage of bed space. Whether the lack of a marriage certificate had any effect on that decision was unknown.

The only problem with having the cell painted was the fumes. We smoked cigarettes to get rid of the smell, but it didn't go away for about 24 hours. We made it thru OK though.

When the county sent me here, they misspelled my name. When I tried to get them to change it, they said "Nope, that's what the paper work says." I even showed them my old ID from my 90 days before, but they still wouldn't change it. What a bunch of fools. I had a small fear that I wouldn't get credit for all this time served!

Day 195: July 21, 1991

I found out today that I'd be leaving on Monday morning at 5:30. I assumed that we'd leave that early to beat the heat of the desert. I was able to learn some other facts to be ready for when I arrived at Mountaincrest.

The part of the prison I was moving into had just been vacated by women. I guessed there were lots of open spaces because of that occurrence. The cells were 12 man dorms. I wasn't too happy about that, because I had hoped for a one or two man cell, but it was prison.

There were about a thousand job openings down there because it was so empty. So I thought that I'd at least get a job right away, and get started on my half time. I tried calculating my release date, which came out to be 12-21-91—the day before my birthday.

All of the other information about the place I'd heard was contradictory. Some said it was air-conditioned, others said no way. Some say the yard is nothing but desert, but I didn't believe that. They said it was very hot, and that I believed. However, the cool spell of weather lately made me hope that it would last longer. Like all year.

I'd be doing all I could to get into the clinic there as a worker, with hopes that I'd be able to use my nursing in some way. I felt so ignorant, and like I'd lost so much of my nursing training.

Day 196: July 22, 1991

Daybreak, 5AM—I was awake before the guard ever started knocking on cell doors to wake people up to go to R&R (Receiving & Release). I did the usual routine of wetting down my hair and brushing my teeth. I had tried many times in the past to get my bangs cut, but so far I had not had any luck. It looked so raggedy. I could put my bangs in my mouth, and they didn't give out combs or sell them there. I desperately needed a comb.

5:30AM—Moved to R&R. Twenty of us were being moved to Mountaincrest, and we all filed in to be strip searched and were given a red jumpsuit for the long ride. The jumpsuit was what all enroute prisoners wore when traveling to another prison. They gave us each a box lunch for breakfast—Peanut butter, bread, potato chips, 2 chocolate chip cookies, and a hardboiled egg. (Please realize that no water was available to drink with the peanut butter, so I did without. I would have had a bunch of peanut butter stuck in my throat if I had tried to eat it!)

5:50AM—All 20 of us, having been searched and changed, entered a holding cell. To wait.

6:00AM—A new batch of prisoners began stripping down and getting the same red jumpsuits as we had on. Except something was wrong with these prisoners. Some were constantly moving about (the 'Thorazine Shuffle'), and others were eating everything in site, including the contents of the garbage can that had discarded food from the group that was in the cell before them. In the same group were inmates that just stared off into space, oblivious to their surroundings, and more that were quietly mumbling to themselves. These inmates were all put into the holding cell next to the one I was in, so there was no direct contact. But they were getting on our bus! 4 hours with these goobs?

We all sat there, those in my cell, and thought amongst each other how screwed it was that we were going to have to ride with these weirdos! For four hours! Everybody in our cell had a "deep-in-thought" look on their face. You could've cut the dread in that cell with a knife.

7:30AM—After an hour and a half of sitting, the weirdos finally started to get loaded onto the bus. Since the first prisoners on the bus are loaded into the back seats, that meant they would be in the back of us. We were all uneasy about that, because we wanted to be able to see these guys!

7:45AM—The guards started unloading our cell. I was about #16 to go (out of 20) so I was near the end. To our relief, when we arrived outside, we saw 2 buses. So the nuts weren't traveling with us after all. Phew! We were shackled with a chain on our waist, then placed in handcuffs which were attached to the chain. As I was being shackled by a nice guard named Estrada, the inmate next to me was a Mexican who didn't speak English. I had seen a large abdominal wound, like a stab wound, just a bit over from his belly button and at the same place where the chain was going.

He was wincing, and the lady guard told him to hold still. Well, like the fool I am, I spoke up and said,

"He has an abdominal wound."

Well, my cop didn't like me speaking for someone else, so he yells at me,

"What's the matter? He can't talk for himself? Are you fucking him?"

Obviously, I knew I'd better keep my mouth shut. But the lady cop leans over and says,

"What'd you say? This guy doesn't speak English."

So I repeated it to her, and again this screwball guard Estrada jumps all over my shit. Well, I'm a humanitarian (regardless of my crime), and I thought they should know before they hurt him. Screw the macho guard. Whatever happened to that prisoner, I never found out. I walked on the bus, and they put ankle shackles on. They were really uncomfortable, and the ride ahead was going to be plenty long. I sat down in the only unoccupied seat. The front seat.

79

Now, this bus was like a Greyhound coach, only it consisted of 4 compartments. The first was where the driver and an armed guard sat. The second was a bench along the right side (large enough for 4 inmates) and 3 cages with one 2-man bench in each (for violent or protective custody inmates). The 3rd section was 12 2-man seats on each side of the bus aisle for a total of 24 seats. The rear of the bus was a toilet and in a cage completely separated from the rest of the bus, a spot for another armed guard to sit. The only entrance into this cage is from the outside. The female guard climbed into the back cage with a pump-action 12 gauge shotgun when we left the prison. The guard up front had an AK 14 assault rifle.

We left Inacia City and went to the prison in Solano, just a short drive away. We picked up another inmate from there, and then after Estrada and the female guard had picked up their guns (they had to leave them at the gate of the prison—no guns allowed inside), Estrada went into a big speech.

"Now, you guys fuck with us, and we'll fuck with you. Keep the noise down, and if you want to talk to someone, sit next to him, don't yell across the bus. If you get loud, you're in shackles and I don't have any problem coming back there and slapping the shit out of you. So treat us with respect and we'll treat you with respect. We've got about 3 hours to Mountaincrest, so let's get going and keep the noise down."

Wo. I was so scared by mister dick-head. Well, I figured we would take I-5 south, but instead we headed north towards San Francisco.

9:30AM—We arrived at South Central Penitentiary. Wow, was that place old. It was absolutely archaic. We let off one inmate and picked up 14 others. Now the bus was full, and Estrada says, "4 hours to go to Mountaincrest," and the rest of his bullshit speech he had made earlier.

10:30AM—We left South Central and stopped at a café so the guards could get their lunch, and give us another box lunch. Yep, same as the one before. Same rules applied, so I didn't eat lunch either. That's okay. I wanted to lose a little weight anyway.

11:15AM—We passed Golden Gate Fields (the horse track) and the ride was long and rough on the wrists and ankles. Those shackles really hurt.

3:00PM—We arrived at Mountaincrest, and wouldn't you know it, I get picked out by Estrada to clean the bus. He left the shackles on, and made me stand in front of the bus outside. It was only 105 degrees, and the bus was air conditioned. At least I was in the shade. A cool 98 I guessed. He took off the chain and handcuffs when everyone else was unshackled and off the bus, but he left the ankle cuffs on. So I just swept like they didn't bother me. I think he was stunned that I didn't complain at all, knowing that's what he wanted so he could denounce me some more. I wasn't going to give him the satisfaction of seeing me squirm. He even reminded me of Mindy's ex. What a dick-fuck.

After I finished sweeping out the bus, another inmate got to mop. Then Estrada took our ankle shackles off, and we went and stood in an outside cage. No shade either. 105 degrees hot. We stayed out there for roughly 30 minutes.

3:30PM—We arrived inside a holding cell, and waited for another hour and a half.

5:00PM—They finally decided to feed us. And with good food, too. Of course it wasn't home cooking, but it was better than what we'd been getting at Inacia City. It helped to end my hunger because we were fed a lot. I didn't really want to lose weight anyway.

7:00PM—They started to hand out property that we had been allowed to bring with us from Inacia City. I was third. For some reason, the guard going through my stuff took my lotion bottle and my dental floss. Why was I allowed to purchase these items at Inacia City, a state prison, yet not allowed to have it here in Mountaincrest, also a state prison? I had them pour the lotion in my disposable cup, as I needed it for the remaining sunburn. I was allowed to keep everything else that I had brought from Inacia City. It was interesting to note that some inmates were allowed to keep their dental floss.

9:00PM—They finally took us to our housing unit. I was shocked at the way the housing units were set up. It was a large warehouse, with 24 separate 12-man dorms. These dorms did not have bars on the front of them. Instead, they were open to the main warehouse floor, so inmates could come and go from their bunks to other dorms as they pleased. I didn't like this aspect of the housing unit when I first arrived, but I would adapt over time.

There was an upper and a lower floor. We each had a locker with a combo lock issued by the prison when we received our property.

It was bad enough being in a two-person cell, where the toilet had to be shared while the other inmate turned his head. Now that we had open dorms, all of the inmates in the housing unit shared the toilets. There were two toilet facilities on each floor, which consist of 4 toilets and 2 sinks all in a row. No partitions or walls for any bit of privacy. Then, next to the toilets, there was a row of 8 sinks for oral care and shaving. At least we had metallic mirrors, which we didn't have at Inacia City. They weren't clear, but they were good enough to see yourself.

The dorms were all along the walls in here, and there were 2 TVs with benches in front of them. Then, scattered all over the rest of the floor, were a bunch of tables for writing, or playing cards, or whatever else one wanted to use them for. I'd draw a diagram of the cell, but that might be considered useful for someone who wanted to assist in a breakout from the prison.

10:05PM—One of the first 'better' situations I noticed at Mountaincrest was the ability to take a shower when desired (for the most part). I took a shower after the 10pm count, being sticky and sweaty from the long trip down from Inacia City, and fell asleep fast. I was beat. But I didn't sleep well. I took advantage of the freedom to shower frequently.

11:00PM—So far, the worst part of my transfer, that I was willing to complain about, was not having a comb. My hair was a mess, and there's nothing I could do about it. I really needed another care package.

Day 197: July 23, 1991

I hoped to get a chance at 4:30pm to use the phone and call Mindy. They only had 4 phones for all the 288 inmates in that building. I hoped that most of them didn't have anyone to call.

They served us three hot meals a day at Mountaincrest. The box lunches at Inacia City were always given away, as they were not much, so receiving a hot lunch here was an advantage.

Of the many things I didn't like about Mountaincrest, they gave us brand new pants. I had always hated new clothes and the way they itched. So there I was, gritting my teeth, and wearing the pants only when I had to, like to chow.

I felt that the shackles on our ankles during the transfer bus trip were totally unnecessary. If anyone among us was that much of a threat or escape risk, he didn't belong on the bus.

It was really hot there. I was sitting in my boxers again after just going to lunch. They served macaroni salad, ham and cheese Sandwiches, hash browns, and a banana. They called for seconds, too! Wow. Kinda scary to think a living being would want more of that stuff! I would find that in the days to come, I would be one of those living beings.

Day 198: July 24, 1991

After arriving at Mountaincrest State Prison, I was processed and dumped in dorm #120. I was lucky because the total number of inmates brought into this institution at the same time as me was 34, and only 10 were put into a dorm. 10 were put into "the Hole", the lock down unit. The other 14 were put into the gym, which was used as a halfway point until one was placed in a dorm. As astounded as I was by the ways and appearance of the dorm, I was, at least, happy that I was not stuck in the gym.

While I was on yard #1, I spent my time making a friend out of the gentleman below me. Tim was the first guy I'd met in the system I would refer to as a gentleman.

Tim helped me get my special package slip and informed me of the correct way to fill it out. He also was in the process of getting me a job in the office with him (he was a clerk), but he wasn't able to act quick enough. God bless him for trying.

I attempted to expose myself to the outer elements, those being the heat and sun delivered in the mist of the desert valley where Mountaincrest State Prison was located. But I found that the glare was too intense for my eyes, and without sunglasses, I was getting a headache from standing outside for more than 5 minutes. So I was forced to remain in the dorm, where the swamp coolers kept the temperature down to a comfortable zone, until the sun had set on the horizon, somewhere near 8:00pm. The only other time I would leave the dorm during the day was to go to the mess hall.

I busied myself during the day by reading the novels I had brought with me from Inacia City. And since I was within earshot of the T.V. set, when 10 am came along on weekday mornings, it was time to set the book down and watch a game show.

In so doing, the novel of a mere 450 pages lasted me 7 whole days. It was important to stretch out one's activities during the course of imprisonment so that boredom was kept to a minimum.

After the game show came a series of soap operas. Yes, the convicts watched (with just as much intensity, I might add, as housewives) the soaps. I watched soaps back in 1983 and '84, when Luke and Laura ('General Hospital') were chasing each other, and (on 'Days of our Lives') when Roman was getting killed by Stephano, during my recuperation from my motorcycle accident. I had since gotten into school to study for my nursing degree, and left Luke, Laura, Bo, and Hope behind.

And now I was getting back into them. And on 'All My Children', who should show up but the same actress who played Laura on 'General Hospital' those many years ago. As the world changes, so the world stays the same.

At 8pm, I would go outside and walk around the yard area 10 times. This was the equivalent of 2½ miles, since the perimeter of the yard was a 440 yard course, just as it was at Inacia City. I did this every night, when I was still adjusting to my surroundings.

After I had walked, I would work out a little bit with the elaborate weight set that the CDC provided for its prisoners. I would do a few sets of curls with 105 Lbs. Then I'd grab a 25 Lb disk, and do 50 sit-ups at a 45-degree angle, so the sit-ups really worked my gut. For as long as I could remember, I had wanted to have ripples on my abdomen, and maybe this exercise would work.

Day 200: July 26, 1991

On day 5 in Building #1, I was moved upstairs to a different dorm. I was satisfied by this move because I felt it was a way of saying "Your staying here." Unfortunately, I was incorrect.

Day 202: July 28, 1991

I was told to gather up my property. I was being moved to yard #5. I was upset, downright mad. But I had learned to take anything the system threw at me.

When I was called out to the yard with my property, I found that most of the inmates that had been housed in the gym on Yard #1 were waiting to go to another yard also. I soon learned that we were all going to the same place—Yard #5, the gym.

I was thoroughly disgusted. We stood, or sat, (our choice) in the sun for about 15 minutes before moving out through the gate to wait for roll call. Then we were marched about a quarter of a mile to yard #5, carrying our property with us in the sheets or pillowcases or plastic bags we had used (again our choice) to gather it all together.

When we arrived at the gym, there were a number of tables set up. One by one, the guards were going through our property, looking for contraband. This time, the guard who checked my property took two of my three ink pens and my shoes from Inacia City. He said we were only allowed one pair of boots, and I was wearing my new ones, given to me at clothing exchange the prior Tuesday.

It was clear that the guards had no guidelines to follow when deciding what was allowed and what wasn't. Every time I changed locations, from prison to prison, and even yard to yard, items I was allowed to have at one place where taken from me because they weren't allowed at the next place. It was completely up to the guard doing the search, and probably depended a lot on if he or she had gotten laid the night before. Another lesson learned.

Inside the gym, it was hot and stuffy. The gym had been converted to a 70 bunk, 140 inmate holding tank. Each bunk had a locker, but they were not always side by side. The locker for bed 5 low (the lower bunk) was 30 feet away, whereas my locker for bed 5 up (my bunk) was right next to it.

The toilets were 12 side-by-side and when you sat on one you looked directly out into the gym—no walls. There were 6 sinks near the toilets and 6 sinks on the opposite side of those. In the dorm, there were 4 toilets that faced a wall. At least the dorm offered a little bit of privacy. None was offered in the gym.

Only two telephones hung on the wall in the gym, as compared to the 4 in the dorm. A sign up list still existed, as in the dorm, but contrary to dorm procedures, an inmate was only allowed to use the phone for 15 minutes every 24 hours. The constant change of rules from place to place was irritating, but I realized I had to go with it or lose it. And I had no desire to lose it.

Only one T.V. existed in the gym, and the noise from the rest of the gym made hearing the T.V. all but impossible. Fans were brought in during the night hours, the large 24" diameter "stands-on-a-pole" type. But, during the day, the guards took the fans away so we could sweat all day. Nice!

Day 203: July 29, 1991

I was interviewed for a job as a clerk in the Sergeant's office by his secretary. I took a written test that consisted of spelling, syllable division and punctuation. I achieved 100% on the last two and a 91% on the spelling. For the typing test, I typed 50 wpm, which was a best for me. So I'd been happy since, despite the increasing temperature.

The secretary said she would call me, but since I had applied at another job, I would probably go there, because—get this—I was "top rate." She said that! Careful . . . my ego.

The other job I had applied for was for the Poultry, Industry, and Agriculture secretary job. It paid $68 a month, and was outside the gate. I thought that job would have been more of a challenge for me. I'd have to wait and see if anything came of it.

Day 209: August 4, 1991

I continued to experience those times when emotions ran wild. I tried to adjust to the new life at Mountaincrest. Despite the desert heat, I had started going outside at 2pm to walk 10 laps around the track. My eyes were adjusting to the light, but I still had to squint pretty much the whole time to avoid the headaches from the light. The reason I walked in the afternoon was so I could play volleyball at 6:30 (after dinner). I was on a 5-member team that was pretty good, and I'd always enjoyed volleyball.

After I had finished my ten laps, I went back into the gym, and cooled off by soaking my shirt in water from the water fountain, and then stepping into the shower area (right next to each other) and wringing it out over my head. The showers were at a set temperature, and that temp was above luke warm, but not actually hot or steamy. Anyway, I felt refreshed after that. Without much else to do, I would pick up my book, and continue reading.

I was supposed to call Mindy today at a set time, but I had been trying to get the doctor to allow me to get a pair of prescription sunglasses sent in here. I was in the sick-call line from 7:15am to 10:30am before I was called in to be told that I would be seen next Wednesday! Life in prison sure was fun.

The glare from the sun was giving me headaches, so I had to stay inside way too much for my tastes. The short time out for my daily walk and volleyball was not enough.

I had also signed up for a softball team, even though I had the distinct possibility of becoming the ill-reputable 'dump-truck'. As with an attorney who can't win a case, this also applies to someone who can't hit or catch a ball. I had done well as a hitter in little league in my younger years, but my fielding was never anything to brag about. I could never get over that "Stand in front of the ground ball and block it with your body" idea. The thought of the ball popping up and smacking me in the face kept me from being anything but an outfielder. My attempt to play at Inacia City recently made me wonder if I should even try. Although I wrote to Mindy that I'd "be sure to let (her) know if I earned 'dump-truck' status," I realized that I might be too embarrassed to say anything if I earned that title!

The dates of my letters were even more spaced out now that I was at Mountaincrest, more than it had been when in the county or city jail. Having access to a phone negated the need to write just to maintain my sanity. I loved hearing the sound of Mindy's voice.

Day 210: August 5, 1991

After sitting in the gym for 6 days, I was finally moved to a dorm, still on yard #5, in the morning hours. The dorm was of the same design as the one I was in before, with a couple of changes. Unlike the first dorm I was placed in here at Mountaincrest, my new dorm had limited access to the telephone; I could only talk for 15 minutes a day! The phone calls were monitored fairly regularly, which made any thoughts of talking dirty to Mindy undesirable for both of us.

Another difference between the dorms was that the new one was a quiet dorm. Many of the inmates there had night or early morning jobs, so it was quiet most of the day. That helped when I wanted to take a nap.

The heat in the gym and the light sunburn I received while practicing softball for the first 2 days on the yard gave me the need to sleep about 12 to 14 hours a day. I had treated the sunburn with the aloe vera lotion I was able to keep from Inacia City, and it had healed quickly. Even today, I slept for another 3 hours after getting moved in to my new bed in the new dorm.

I hadn't heard anything about a job yet. I hoped I would get one soon. Mountaincrest, a real prison, not like Inacia City, was a bummer.
The weather was pretty mild now that I was out of the gym. Of course, that's Murphy's Law. I found it amazing how every single inmate I met with a goatee beard was such an asshole! Just like a guy I met last April in Inacia City, every one of them seemed to have their heads up their ass. Guess "birds of a feather," right?

The softball team I was on was called the Outlaws. We played different teams from our yard according to a schedule set by the officers. Today, the warden spoke to all of the coaches at a meeting, "All teams must be racially balanced. That means for every 4 whites, there must be 4 blacks, and 2 Mexicans." Ah, quotas, even in prison on prison yard softball teams. Makes an American proud that we've come so far since the Civil War.

The warden's speech gave me reason to consider quitting the softball team. I hated racial shit, and his speech made me think that the warden's head was stuck in his rectal sphincter.

Day 213: August 8, 1991

I decided to continue on the team, despite having a glove issued to me by the prison that was barely able to fit on my hand. At yesterday's practice, I was sunburned pretty intensely. We practiced softball today, and I added to the sunburn. I can really be a smart guy when I want to. Little blisters, about the size of a pimple, showed up on my shoulders! I wasn't in any pain, and I still had some aloe vera lotion left, so I was able to sooth the sunburn without being in any discomfort. I hoped that my supply would last until the following Thursday, when I would go to canteen.

The weather continued to remain mild, not getting uncomfortably hot for the last 3 days, which made it easy to not realize I was burning in the sun. I stayed inside most of the afternoon unless we had softball practice. By design, most of our games were played at night after dinner to avoid the distressing heat of the afternoon.

Today, we played a practice game against another team. I played shortstop. I amazed myself. I actually did pretty good. I would continue to avoid 'Dump-Truck status' as long as possible. I also hit all 3 times I was at bat, and one was a home run!

I had decreased myself to one cigarette per day, and I had made up my mind that I didn't even want that. The thought of smoking another cigarette was becoming less and less appealing. But I was still fat, and I just couldn't seem to make the flab around my waist go away.

I was called into the Sergeant's office today, at 6:30pm (after dinner). They didn't tell me why, just to go to the Sergeant's office. I didn't know why he would want to see me. Did he have legal mail for me? Did I receive an emergency phone call? Did I do something wrong?

When I arrived at the Sergeant's office, 7 others were also outside. Phew, I thought; it was only legal mail. What else could it be? So I waited outside for a while, as one by one, an inmate was called in to receive his mail. Four went in and came out. Then the last 3, the two and me, were called inside and seated. Then the Sergeant came in and asked us for our ID cards. The he called us into his office separately. Why? To interview us for a job! I was told that it was between an Italian and me. The only thing against me was my Caucasian skin.

Sound like something I went through before? Yep. I was amazed at how much special treatment that minorities received in prison simply to keep the race card from being played. The interview was short, with a typing test and a few written questions.

When the interview was done, I asked if there was a possibility of getting a textbook sent in here so I could brush-up on my nursing. But this system has no intention of rehabilitating anyone. They just put us here and hold us. I was told I could not get a textbook delivered to me in this prison because they don't allow hardcover books. So, I would lose some of the skills I had learned before I got into this mess, and that would increase the chances of me not being able to find a job, or get good grades in school. What a terrific system, I thought to myself.

Day 220: August 15, 1991

I went outside, sat down on the grass in the center of the yard, and watched the sunset. It was the first sunset I had viewed since arriving at Mountaincrest, and it was breathtaking. The western sky was covered in patchy, fluffy clouds that glowed an iridescent blend of bright red, orange, and lavender. Between myself and the coastal mountains north of San Luis Obispo stood only the barbed wire cyclone fences (there were 2 fences roughly 20 feet apart). These mountains being roughly 75 miles away made for a picture perfect scene, accentuated by the cool ocean breeze that blew in just as the sun peeked behind the mountain range, igniting the sky in a shower of yellow streaks, blazing through the clouds like a spider's web. I sat until the sun was well below the mountains and the first stars had appeared. It was this time that gave me the inspiration to write one of my better poems while locked up, titled "Today the Wind Blew."

Today,
The Wind Blew,
And as my hair whisked from my neck,
I thought of you.
The clouds that rolled over the sky
Brought comfort to my lonely heart.
In my mind,
I envisioned how the moisture held in those clouds waited for the
moment
To be free from the jail that held them captive in the sky.
Just as I long for the day when I can crush the walls that separate
you and I.
And hold you, naked, next to me.
The birds struggled to remain overhead
And their songs caused me to dream of the many wonderful songs
you have given to me,
As the reason for me to continue on
Until at last we become as one.
I cried a tear for us today, because
Today,
The Wind Blew.

Day 227: August 22, 1991

It was my dad's birthday. Spending the time away from him led to
some emotions, and I was working hard to keep my spirits up. I went
to eat lunch and when I sat down with my tray, I looked at the lunch
meat, the beans, the stale cookies, and the brown (wilty) coleslaw
and gagged. I threw it all away and went back to the dorm without
eating anything.

Instead of getting easier to be locked up, I was experiencing more
and more frustration as the time went by. I didn't have a job yet,
and that was a big part of my discontent. My depression led me to
believe I would probably be there the whole term without a job.

I picked up a book from the library on electronics, deciding that I was
going to try to learn something in there. I'd always wondered what

on ohm was. So I'd been going through the book just like I would if I had been in school. Odd, though. This book was hard-covered, the kind they said I couldn't have.

Day 231: August 26, 1991

In prison, the other inmates could be so negative that it would make the average person cringe. When watching a TV show, if an old lady was hit by a car, most inmates around me would say something like, "Yea, that fucked her up!" I would just look at them and think, "What a bunch of jerks."

While an occasional showing of emotion was displayed, the majority of the inmates were so afraid to show any soft emotions that they did the usual "Boo-Hoo" to hide their true feelings. You know; they say "boo-hoo" sarcastically so the way they really feel was hidden from those around them.

I bought 2 six packs at canteen last week, and I decided to wait until Friday, Saturday, and Sunday nights to enjoy one. On Saturday night, I tried something different. Last weekend, I merely poured the Pepsi into a glass over the ice I had received, which was distributed by the guards for the heat, and drank it that way. But it didn't taste right. I figured it was due to the frost on the ice.

So last night, I borrowed an empty Bugler can, received my issue of ice (1 full bugler can), and placed the can of Pepsi inside it, like an ice chest. I thought, "Now the Pepsi is ice cold, I won't need to mix it with that shitty tasting ice, and the Pepsi will taste good." Much to my surprise, it still tasted strange! I guess my taste buds had been without it for so long that my preference for Pepsi had changed. Tonight I did the same as last night with the ice and Pepsi, and it tasted better to me.

I had been lifting weights for the last two weeks. I had increased the weight I was curling from 30 to 40 pounds with dumbbells, and I'd injured my right bicep. It felt like a cramp that wouldn't go away. I thought I was ready for the increase in weight, but I had forgotten to warm-up before the lifting session. I had just walked up and started curling without stretching.

Another fantastic tale was told to me on the baseball field, and the inmate who told me the tale actually expected me to believe him. I just listened, and after he was done with the story, I had only one thing that I wanted to do. I won't mention what that was.

It started when a foul ball from the softball game knocked an inmate unconscious. The inmate had his back turned to the field, and the stray ball caught him in the back of his head. He got hit pretty hard; I saw his feet fly up in the air! Anyways, this inmate next to me starts telling me the story.

"Well, that guy will get some time off for that! He'll get some cash, too. When I was in Tracy (State Pen), a guy broke his ankle while he was playing volleyball, and he had 6 months taken off his sentence and was given $12,000."

I couldn't believe the inmate was so stupid as to believe that. Just another example of the mentality that prevailed in the environment I was in. Or did that really happen? I should have learned by then that anything could happen in prison.

They closed the yard early this evening. I heard that two other yards were on lock-down because of fighting. There had been Crips vs Bloods fights since last week when somebody got stabbed. I was glad I was white!

I was intrigued by the electricity book I had checked out from the library. I was learning the answers to questions that I'd had for years, but never really understood. My brother had tried to teach me the solutions, but his knowledge of electronics was so sophisticated that I couldn't comprehend what he was telling me. I thought I'd be able to finish the book (22 units) in another week, for a total of 2 weeks. Since I was unsure if nursing was a realistic option after my conviction, I decided to focus on learning a new trade.

Day 233: August 28, 1991

I was diligent in finishing the electricity book, even going as far as to take notes on what I'd been learning. I had made my way to Chapter 15, and I was able to apply some of the algebra and trigonometry I'd learned in the past to the equations that were used to find voltage, wattage, current (amperage), and resistance (ohms). I was really enjoying it, and all the studying (about 3 to 4 hours a day) made the time fly by. I was finally learning about all this useful stuff that I'd always been interested in, but never thought that I could really get to understand. I was starting to feel that I should have taken up electrical classes instead of nursing. I hoped I'd be able to learn enough before I was released, to start up some classes and get a degree in electronics if I found out that I couldn't get my RN license.

Day 239: September 3, 1991

When Saturday morning came along, I was not well rested. Friday and Saturday were late-nights, with the TVs on until 2:30am, and I was late in getting to bed. The phones were not on after 10pm. All day Saturday, I was trying to take a nap, but I just couldn't get to sleep. I was tired, but restless.

I was really surprised that this place would do anything special for the inmates, but they organized a five event contest between the four dorm houses in celebration of Labor Day.

I was given the impression that the games were played on all of the yards (6) here at Mountaincrest State Prison, and I actually had a good time! I participated in the sack race, which I came in second, only because the guy that beat me cheated. He didn't go all of the way to the end of the first lap before turning around.

I also tried the sled pull, where a piece of metal with 200 Lbs on it was to be pulled 40 feet. I was really doing great until I slipped! I got up, took about 5 more steps, and slipped again! And I slipped and fell a third time! God I was pissed! Some guy yelled from the side lines,

"Hey, you're spending more time on your ass than on your feet!" He was right, so I had to laugh!

The two events I didn't try were the 3-legged race, and the softball-under-the-chin-pass-it-to-the-next-guy-under-his-chin-as-fast-as-you-can-race! It was pretty wild watching those guys get real close to each other's faces when they passed the ball. No hands!

The last event was the tug-of-war. 20 guys from each house on each team, with a semi-final heat, and then a final heat between the two semi-final heat winners. It was a real blast! Our dorm won! It was a real boost to moral for everyone that got involved in it.

They kept points on it all, and our dorm came in second. I walked away surprised at how good I felt. When I came back inside, I took a little shower, played a few games of cribbage, and then fell asleep with no problem. The next morning came late, and I felt quite rested.

Day 245: September 9, 1991

After being hot for the last few days, the weather had cooled off and everyone was hoping it would stay cool for the winter. I had been told that it would get quite cold there in the winter, about 20° F at night.

Day 246: September 10, 1991

I was playing a game a game of cards when I was called up to the front desk. I was given a pass to the Lieutenant's office, so I walked on over. When I arrived there, a line of inmates was at the window where packages are given out. There was a list on the wall describing what was being distributed, so I took a look, and sure enough my name was on there for a "Care Package"! I had to trot back to my dorm and grab a pillowcase to carry all of the articles I'd received. When I was in my housing unit (510), I asked the guard if I was to <u>see</u> the Lieutenant or if I was just given the pass to get my package. He told me that I was to see the Lieutenant (the pass) <u>and</u> pick up my stuff.

Earlier in the day, I had talked with a guy who knew the secretary of the Program Administrator, the top position of the guards. She was the one who gave me the typing test last month. He said he had worked for her and had developed a good repertoire with her. I asked him to inquire about the possibility of me getting a job. So I followed him over to her office, which was also the Lieutenant's office. He was only inside for a couple of minutes before he came back out and told me, "She can't find your test. She doesn't know you exist." So, she said I should have the officer in my housing unit call her tomorrow at 9am, because it was too late for her to help me then (it was 3:30pm). She would retest me tomorrow.

2000 inmates in that facility, and I got lost in the shuffle! No wonder I'd been passed up for a job by other inmates. At least that mystery was solved. It wasn't because they needed a minority worker, it wasn't because I had only a short time to serve. It was because no one in the office even knew my name. Or so I thought.

I picked up my care package, and took it back to my bed. Then I returned to the office to talk to the Lieutenant.

When I walked in to the Lieutenant's office, I noticed my test (from last month) on his desk. I figured the secretary had found it after I had asked about it yesterday.

He told me that I was top on his list to be his clerk because I was the most qualified for the job. The only thing against me was my short time left. But he was going to try to get me a job as his clerk, as opposed to the Sergeant's clerk job I had been hoping for.

The Lieutenant's Clerk position was a good job. I would be working a morning shift. I was thoroughly pleased, and attempted to shake his hand on the way out. However, contact between a guard and inmate was not allowed.

At last, I might have a job!

Day 247: September 11, 1991

When 9am came this morning, I asked the dorm officer if he would call the secretary for me. I, at least, wanted to thank her for getting me in to see the Lieutenant so quickly. I was actually allowed to use the officer's phone, and she informed me that she had nothing to do with my meeting with the Lieutenant. The Lieutenant had kept my test from the time I had taken it, and he had not forgotten about me!

In the interview, he told me I would get a call within the next couple of days. If I were to get that job, by my calculations, I'd be singing a new song: "I'll be Home for Christmas"!

The weather really cooled off over the next week, and I froze my butt off at night because the vent in my dorm was right over me! What was a blessing when it was hot was now pure hell incarnate. I had to bundle up at night because it seemed like the nights were going to stay on the cold side.

I had received a job description after I was interviewed for by the Lieutenant for the clerical job. The job title was Program Lieutenant's Clerk. The hours were from 6:30am to 2:30pm, Saturday through Wednesday.

To work in the officer's office, inmates were required to maintain a minimum grade 3 level of work performance as defined on the CDC-101 Work Performance Report, report to work on time each day, observe all health and safety regulations and codes, maintain tool and material control, adhere to institution rules, maintain a clean working environment, and follow the instructions of your supervisor and if uncertain of responsibilities, ask your supervisor for instructions. I was also alerted that I might be called in on emergency situations.

Inmates were expected to perform their assigned tasks diligently and conscientiously, and were not to pretend illness or otherwise evade attendance in their assigned work and program activities. Failure to comply with the above duties and responsibilities could result in disciplinary action and/or no work credit for time in non-compliance.

I would be directly responsible to the Program Lieutenant for all unclassified disciplinary paperwork. I would also be responsible for contributing to the smooth operation of the clerk's office.

Unlike most of the inmates I met each day, I didn't look for trouble or try to be a tough-guy. I had consciously avoided any situation while I had been incarcerated that might lead to an altercation.

After I started work as the Lt.'s Clerk, no inmate ever messed with me that I could recall. It was like having a position of power. Overnight, every inmate on Yard #5 knew that I was the guy to go to if he needed something from the Lieutenant.

Day 248: September 12, 1991

I was told today by a Sergeant that the position for the Lt's Clerk had been filled. Needless to say, I was pretty pissed off that, again, I'd been overlooked for a job, more than likely because of my skin color. Didn't the Lieutenant say I was the most qualified for the job? I went from a great day on Monday to this shit-hole day today. Some things never change, and I guess shit just comes naturally in prison.

Day 254: September 18, 1991

Welcome to "The Lighter Side of Prison."

An inmate went to his visit one day, where visits between inmates and friends/family are encouraged. Only today the encouragement of a surprise visit got this inmate in trouble.

He knew his son's mother, his past girlfriend, was coming to visit him this morning. So it was not at all unusual to hear him say, "Oh, shit!" when his wife greets him instead of his ex-girlfriend!

Trying to hide the fear that the woman of his future and present would meet the woman of his past in a place that he couldn't get away from, this guy knew he was in deep do-do. You see, the girls of his life didn't like each other. Let me rephrase that; they hated each other.

So when the ex-girlfriend did show up, the wife went off. He tried to calm her, but she was like a wet hen—pissed!

So, ladies; if you want to go visit your boyfriend in prison, and you don't want to run into one of his other girlfriends, I suggest not surprising him. It could turn out to be a surprise he'd rather do without!

I received legal mail today. Legal mail had to be opened by the officers and inspected for contraband before the inmate can have it, but the officer cannot read the material. All of the other letters were scanned by officers to make sure that no escape plans were being included in the contents.

The legal mail I had received came in the form of an 8 ½" x 11 ½" x 4" box. Inside were the complete transcripts of my jury trial, sent to me by my lawyer who was working on my appeal. This box was sealed shut with strapping tape. You know, the tape that you can pick up a car with? The guards here were trying to get the box open to inspect the contents, but since no scissors or knives are allowed, they were having a difficult time cutting thru the tape. They tried their keys and their ballpoint pens, but could only get a small hole made in the tape. Then they proceeded to try to rip the tape in half.

All this time I was watching, and it occurred to me that they were going about it all wrong. So I asked, "Can I try?" to the guard. He stepped back, as if to say, "Go for it, Smart-ass." I grabbed the end of the tape, and pulled the tape off, and the box fell open! The guard looked so pathetic, I guess box-opening wasn't taught in guard school! The other guard tried to hide his laughter.

Day 258: September 22, 1991

I was scheduled to meet with my counselor and find out when my new release date was on October 10th. Hopefully it would be December 10th or close to it! I was anxious to find out when I'd be back together with Mindy, and out of this hell-hole.

Today I had to listen to a couple of inmates talking more of their bullshit lies. They were conspiring against one of the female guards here, saying she's unfair, which basically means she won't put up with their shit.

The days seemed endless at times when the work load in the office was low. To fill the time one day, I typed a poem to Mindy around the outside of a regular 8 ½" by 11" piece of paper. As I came to the end of the paper, I'd remove the entire piece and turn it 90 degrees so that the next sentence followed the previous sentence in a 'Round About' way. Each time I arrived at the starting point of the first line, I would space down one line and continue typing around and around. I called it my "Round About Letter." The things I did to entertain myself and keep my sanity . . .

Day 259: September 23, 1991

Today was my first full day of work as the Lt's Clerk, and what a day! I was not doing much until after 12 noon when I was handed a steady flow of work order forms and disciplinary documents. They all had to be typed, in carbon copies (5), which meant they had to be done near perfect! I was really nervous; fixing a carbon copy error was tough.

The Sergeant gave me a 154 (Bed move) form to type up. He had made an error on it, though. It was a medical move for an inmate with a hurt leg. 139u (upper) was going to 172L (lower) and visa-versa. Well, he had written 139u to 172l and 172l to 172l. Oops, but I caught it, did it the correct way, and showed it to him for his approval. He was really glad I caught the mistake! Yea! One point for me on my first day of work.

One of the Sergeant's clerks was a conceited ass who thought he was pretty smart. He told me that he was a Post Graduate student, meaning he had a four-year degree. I thought it odd that he didn't say what his degree was in. We bumped heads a little bit, being that he wanted to show me he was the "Alpha Male" of the office. I just laughed inside. He reminded me of the saying, "A smart man never has to tell anyone that he's smart."

I had encountered one problem. Since the showers don't open until 7am each morning, and I reported to work at 6:30 each morning, I would be showing up to work without a shower.

I spoke to the Lieutenant about my problem, and I was given a note to give to the dorm guards on my first day that gave the guards permission to let me take a shower each morning when I woke up. Not only did I get to take a shower in the morning, but I didn't have to compete with any other inmate for the use of the shower. Nice perk!

The food at Mountaincrest was getting bad. I had not been eating very much lately; it was that bad. A few inmates were sick all week from food poisoning! I was practically surviving on candy bars and almonds from my care package.

Day 266: September 30, 1991

I received my sunglasses today, and they were a good fit. I could finally go outside and enjoy the sun without squinting liked an Eskimo.

My job was going well. I seemed to be holding my own with the other guards in the office, and I was now getting along with the other clerks, even the one who was so brash on my first day on the job.

I started playing the piano to accompany the choir in the chapel, but decided not to pursue that. I was uncomfortable around the other convicts attending the service, who were punks on the street, and now, in there, they were repentant sinners who preached the bible like they understood it!

The preacher, actually just the inmate that led the service, asked me yesterday if I had "thanked the Lord for putting me in here", here being prison. I looked at him and plainly stated, "No." He tried to recite some passage in Hebrews that we should thank the Lord for delivering us to where he sends us.

Oh, Screw Me! It's that type of stupidity that has made me so uncomfortable in a church. And then he went on to say something about Satan, and I left. I decided for myself long ago that the idea of Satan was not part of my belief system. Satan was invented by man because man needed a reason to explain why bad things happened. When a lion kills an antelope for food, is that bad? Bad things happen, but not because "the devil made me do it." Bad things happen, period.

Day 269: October 3, 1991

I stayed rather busy at work today. The Lieutenant had asked me to type up a memo that was written by an inmate. It was the minutes to an advisory committee for the inmates, and it was 9 pages long. Of course, I had to keep correcting grammar, spelling, etc., because the convict who wrote it was a blithering idiot.

When I got back to my bunk from work, after typing the memo (four full pages typed), it was after 4pm! I was supposed to get off at 2:30pm, but I was doing my job.

At the very end of my shift, I was handed a form of paper. On it, I found out my release date from the prison: December 12, 1991. Merry Christmas.

Day 273: October 7, 1991

I tried giving the piano playing for the church a second try, but they were so unorganized, I lost track of time. I again made the decision to quit, because it wasn't any fun for me. Since I'm white, and almost all of the rest of them were black, they wouldn't listen to me.

Day 276: October 10, 1991

It was relatively busy for most of the day. And since I was counting down the hours I had left there (it was 6pm and that left 1,501 hours until departure), anything that could make the days whiz by a little faster was good.

I couldn't believe that it had been 10 months since I last held Mindy in my arms. Well, 2 more months and nothing would ever come between us again!

Day 278: October 12, 1991

Today was cool. A group of outsiders came to our yard and put on a show for us. It went on all day today (I think there were three 1/2 hour shows). I caught a tiny bit of the first one this morning. It was a guy who must have weighed about 350 Lbs! He was about 5'10", so you can imagine the size of the guy! His forearms were 17" around! I didn't hear how big his upper arms were.

Anyway, this guy, for our (the inmates) entertainment, puts a nail through a 2x4 board, with his hand! He just held the nail like it was a needle, and poked it through the board with one quick thrust! Serious power!

Then he power-lifted (deep knee bend with weights on his shoulders) with 660 Lbs! Wow! Then he had an inmate hit him as hard as he could (the inmate) in his stomach. It didn't even phase the guy! He ended the show by saying how some guys think that if you believe in Jesus Christ, then you're a sissy. Or you're weak. He dared anyone to say that he was a weak sissy!

Work was busy for me today. I decided to remake the example book of the forms I typed up, such as the CDC-115. The examples in the book were now old and outdated. So I had taken it upon myself to update all of the examples. It was taking a long time, exactly what I had hoped for. I hoped it would take me until next Sunday to finish. The week had gone by fast so far, with all the work I'd focused on.

1368 hours left. Or so I thought.

Day 283: October 17, 1991

I'd really done it. I had blown the chance of spending Christmas with Mindy. It was all so surreal, and happened so fast, I couldn't believe it.

Last week, I had written a letter to the Sergeant of Yard Five. I told him that an inmate in our dorm was playing his stereo all night and someone was going to kick his butt. I couldn't be specific in my letter as to who was going to hurt who because that would be "snitching", and I knew how that would be looked at by the inmates.

I had actually stopped another inmate from smashing the radio down on the radio's owner's face while he slept. I had awaked to see the inmate ready to do it and said, "No, man, that won't do anything but hurt you." So he just shut it off and went back to bed. The Sergeant thought my note was a threat.

Now I was in the "hole". It was very fucked up—I couldn't believe this had happened! The Sergeant told me that I should have socked-up the guy after he refused to turned down his radio. I couldn't understand why officials there condoned violence. It just didn't make any sense.

I had no idea how long I'd be there in solitary confinement. I didn't know if the CDC-115 for "Threatening an Inmate" would hold up, either. And I didn't know for sure if my job was history! What I did know was that this type of infraction would cost me my good time. I wasn't going to be home for Christmas.

I was now on 24 hour lockdown. It really sucked. I was now without access to a phone, so I couldn't talk to Mindy. I felt like such an idiot, thinking the cops there would want to avoid violence!

Day 289: October 23, 1991

I spent eight days in "The Hole". The Lieutenant was out on some vacation time that very week, and thus he couldn't have known what had transpired while he was gone.

The timing of my detention and placement in "The Hole", the first day of the Lieutenant's vacation, led me to believe that the Sergeant who ordered my detention had planned it that way. And I had written the letter six days earlier, plenty of time for the Sergeant to have reacted to it before then. The day he returned to work and learned of my segregation, he ordered my release.

Day 290: October 24, 1991

What a crazy life . . . Being thrown into "the hole" was the worst thing that could've happened to me. The thoughts that ran through my head as I laid on my bunk in that small cell with the loud mouth jerk I had to share the 10 x 6 cell with were all but unthinkable. But those same thoughts were important to understand what happens when the shit gets real bad.

I thought of Mindy constantly. I had to do some very hard concentrating to not lose it. The thought that I had messed up my chance to spend Christmas with her had me freaking out. After all the sweating I'd done about getting a job, and then getting my ½ time credits applied, I was feeling like I was finally losing control.

I hadn't asked God for much of anything since I was imprisoned. Not from lack of faith, but because it wasn't how I thought. Many people ask God for favors every day, and when they come true, or happen, that person feels blessed. But when the favor does not happen, they say, "God must not have heard me," or, "I have been a bad person lately." I don't believe that God grants favors, so when I pray to him, I do my best not to ask him for anything. God helps those who help themselves.

This time, however, I did ask him to help me get out of this mess. I asked that the CDC-115 would be dropped. Imagine my surprise when I found out it had been dropped!

I was so happy to get out of that place, I wanted to jump for joy. Upon returning to Yard #5, I found out that I still had my job, and I was ecstatic! The sun felt so good. To be able to stretch out, and breath the air. I couldn't wait to be really free again.

I returned to work as if nothing had happened. I returned to the job I'd started of fixing up the example book. The Lieutenant had decided to start having me type up "Closure Letters". Those letters referred to felony cases not taken by the D.A. that had occurred inside the prison, usually violent attacks of one inmate upon another.

When they had locked me up in "The Hole", the officer who cleaned out my locker didn't know I had white shorts. They were on top of my boxers, and the officer inadvertently took them and gave them to the clothing exchange, along with the rest of my state issued clothes. So the shorts were gone for good. However, it was cooling off, so I wouldn't be needing them.

Day 295: October 29, 1991

I didn't understand why, but I had been unable to contact Mindy on the phone, and I hadn't received a letter from her for a few weeks. The constant talk by other inmates that she'd be gone by the time I was released from prison stressed me out to the point of depression. As it turned out, she was busy with her new job, and trying to lock down a place for us to live together after my release, which was coming up in just over a month, if I didn't lose my ½ time.

I received some good news today from the Sergeant. He informed me that: A) I had been given 'S' time while in the "hole;" and (B) the paperwork would say that I was thrown in the "hole" by mistake! An error on their (the officer's) part! I was even paid for the days I missed! A paid vacation in prison! How's that for status?

Day 301: November 4, 1991

39 days to go.

Day 306: November 9, 1991

I received this letter from my dad. I had always felt ashamed of being a convict and shaming the good name of my family. It was my sincerest hope to someday make my father proud of me. This letter confirmed that he was still the wonderful father he had always been.

"I will start this letter today, but I doubt that I shall finish it this week. There are lots of things to be covered and I have given a lot of thought to what they shall be. As your release date fast approaches, I know you are looking forward to it with great anticipation and excitement. I do not want to dampen that spirit, but I do want you to come out of prison with your eyes open. You must know what lies ahead for you and what you must do to get your life back on track. The following are some factors you must recognize and deal with daily once you are back home:

1. You have been convicted of a felony and incarcerated. You cannot change that simple truth. Certain doors that you formerly took for granted as being open to you will be closed. We do not know whether or not your nursing career is still a viable option for you. It may be . . . it may not be. Friends of the past will not be friends of the future. Prepare yourself to be ostracized from many social activities. You will find it necessary to make a new life, with new friends. It is your decision about what you tell people concerning what has happened to you the past year. You can make up a fictitious past to cover it, you can sidestep it as long as you can or you can tell the truth outright. The decision must be yours, but remember what an awful lot of politicians have learned, i.e., lies have a way of coming back to haunt you;

2. You are not abandoned. There are many of us here who love you and still care for you very deeply. We will be here for you when you need us. Do not feel any reluctance or hesitation to come to any of us when you are in need—regardless of what that need may be;

3. You must focus the blame for what has happened to you on one person—YOU. It is imperative that you accept this fact, put it behind you and get on with your life. Do not attempt to minimize what you did to that man. Do not attempt to

rationalize that there was any justification for what you did to him. You must accept that what you did was wrong in the eyes of our society and it that society in which you must now make your new life. You were wrong. The instant you crossed your doorstep to go after that man outside your house, you were wrong. You were not acting rationally. No matter how angry you become, you cannot cross that line from a civilized person to an uncivilized person. You crossed that line by yourself. No one made you do it. You did it entirely on your own. Your have paid dearly for that brief moment of unclear thinking and poor judgment. What caused you to do it? Alcohol? Drugs? Rage? Fear? A combination of any or all of these things? Only you can sort it out and determine how you can prevent such a thing from happening again. And sort it out you must, for anything remotely close to this must <u>NEVER</u> happen again;

4. You will have to divorce yourself of any need for, or possession of, any type of weapon on your person, in your car, in your place of domicile, etc. It will probably be a condition of your probation, but you must take the ban on weapons a step further: There must not be even an inference of a weapon (gun, knife, BB gun, slingshot, baseball bat, axes, lead pipe, etc.) in your proximity. You cannot allow yourself to be intimidated into violating even the spirit of your parole. You will have to devise a contingency plan for that day when the man you assaulted confronts you, albeit verbal or physical. In such a circumstance, there is absolutely nothing degrading about turning tail and departing the scene post haste. This is definitely no time to be "cool" or "macho" or any other manly-type of action you formerly would have deemed acceptable. Times have radically changed and you must adjust accordingly.

I am certain there are many things set forth above with which you do not agree. Once you get home, we can discuss them. Nevertheless, I feel that they are all things to which you must give concerted thought during your remaining days behind prison walls. Think about where you are and where you hope to go in the future. Reflect on those around you and how limited are many of their options. Set realistic, short-term goals for 1992 to give you a direction in which to proceed. We will be there to help you.

Love, Dad"

Day 307: November 10, 1991

I found myself having violent thoughts in the days preceding my release from that place called Mountaincrest State Prison. I had been forced to divert my thinking away from the ideas of killing and assault to the point of death upon some of the inmates there. I didn't understand why I was suddenly thinking that way, but the thought patterns were disturbing to me. I had done my best to keep my personal self above the low-life scum that thrived inside of those walls of barbed wire, and until recently, the last week, I had felt on top of the situation. Now, it was obvious that the stress of leaving was getting to me.

I had the continuing feeling that Mindy was drifting away from me. This was happening now, after she had spent 10 months of saying how much she missed me and desired me. She had continued to do all of the things I had asked of her, such as sending the quarterly package that the inmates in the CDC were allowed, sending me a picture (although only one), and writing to me every week. Now, when I called her, she was distant. The enthusiasm was gone from her voice, or so it seemed to me. She no longer wrote to me as often as she had in the past.

I was confused beyond my wildest dreams. Yet, I had been able to explain to myself what may be taking place. I had to rationalize the situation or I would surely go insane.

The pattern of Mindy's actions may simply be the result of her feelings of guilt over my being here, instead of her or Bob. If that was correct, then the rest of the mysterious events taking place with thirty days left until my return home were understandable.

If she had been acting in the premise that I would feel better during my time locked up thinking that she would be there for me when I was released, then I could see her going through the motions she had for the past year.

But now with my impending release, the time had come to let me down easy. She may indeed have spent the past year just doing all she could to keep my faith up, and to keep me believing that I had a reason to stay alive.

I hoped that what I had conjured up in my mind was only unbased falsehoods. I had no desire to have my heart broken again, as so many times before I had experienced the pain of being denied.

After what I had been through up to that point in time, I didn't think I could take it. But I made up my mind. Regardless of what would happen, I would not contemplate suicide. The only alternative would be to push on with what I had left in life.

And that was not going to be much anymore, unless I was extremely lucky and hit some type of jackpot at Tahoe, or in the California Lottery. I planned to move to the Midwest, to try to finish my nursing school, and to obtain my license as a nurse, if that was possible.

I had forgotten a great deal of what I had learned in the 6 years prior to my extended absence from college. I hoped I could get it all back. I was never a great student, having trouble applying myself. Even concentrating on studying for long periods of time was difficult, and now, there was a new problem.

And this one was not mental. It was physical. In the past two weeks, I had developed a muscle-spasm, a twitch in my left eye, in the bottom outside corner. This was located on the opposite side of my face that was smashed almost 9 years ago in my motorcycle accident, and I am at a loss as to what could be causing the twitch, except to add it to my list of pre-release stress symptoms.

My underarms had become agitated by some unknown agent. I was experiencing a typical allergic reaction, with pealing of the axillary skin tissue and irritation, persistent with a rash.

However, no bleeding had occurred with the excoriation, and there was no redness of the skin. I had not changed soap or deodorant. I was hoping that this was a psychosomatic reaction, and in attempts to identify the problem, I had stopped using the deodorant. The irritation had decreased somewhat since stopping with the deodorant stick, so I continued to not use it.

Day 309: November 12, 1991

Yesterday was pretty screwed. I went over to get the container (a big plastic bowl) filled up with coffee. Somebody from the office would go to the kitchen next door, and the workers over there would fill it up for us, so we'd have coffee while we worked. It was mainly for the officers, but we (the clerks) were able to have it also. Well, the guy who filled it up for me didn't fill it up to the top, and he didn't fill the sugar bowl up full either. So I returned to the office, and the other clerks asked me why they (the bowls) weren't filled to the top?

I answered,

"Because that is all they gave me, and I wasn't going to ask for more. I think they're doing us a favor giving it to us in the first place."

Well, about that time, an officer walked into the office and reiterated what I said. He made it clear that the Program Administrator use to drink coffee out of the pot in our office. But due to it being too strong for her tastes (and mine too), she now had her own coffee maker in her office. This coffee pot would be taken away at the first sign of conflict.

These butt-heads decided that I was talking like a cop. They somehow decided that in what I said I had meant that "inmates don't have a thing coming."

Where, or when, the hell did I say that? Crap if I know, but I was pretty pissed off that they would decide they were so intellectual that they could find meaning in a simple sentence that even I didn't know was there! That place was so messed up, and I wouldn't be looking back once I left.

Today, I had a talk with the other clerk, Mike, who was involved in slandering me yesterday, and he reiterated that I had implied that "Inmates don't have a thing coming." I let him know that I didn't say anything of the sort, and he should not analyze what I say. Everything seemed to be okay between us after that.

Mike was definitely smarter than most inmates I'd met, that was for sure. Unfortunately, he had been locked up enough times, in his 42 years, so that he had developed the "convict attitude". That was the attitude that I refused to develop.

A "convict attitude" was a way of life for people in there. It consisted of numerous ideals of living.

There was the "I Hate Cops" syndrome. Any sympathy to an officer or an authority figure of any kind was perceived as wrong and disgraceful. "The only good cop is a dead cop," was one phrase I'd heard countless times since my imprisonment. This way of thinking, I felt, was both antisocial and immature.

There was the "Steal From Anyone." This included mom, dad, brother, sister, best friend, or other person that one knows. The rule was to steal anything not tied down. From sugar packets to spoons to sheets of paper to manilla folders to ink pens to coffee. Steal it all, especially if it was state owned, like the material in the office. And I'd been chastised by other inmates here because I wouldn't steal for them. But they were too stupid to understand my way of thinking.

There was the "Respect Me" disposition. Of course, around here it only went one way. The punks in there wanted to be respected without giving any respect out first. The officers were often attacked under this phrase, that "I (the inmate) don't have to respect you because you disrespected me first." Usually, though, the officer has not been the first to be disrespectful, but since all of his buddies would side with him (the inmate), of course he would tell his partners that the cop disrespected him first.

There was the "Fight, Don't Talk" mood. Any and all differences around there were settled by fists. Even the officers admonished it. It was the way 'men' handled things. After being told this by a few officers, I came to realize that it was no wonder that inmates who came into this system stayed in the system. They were taught to assault someone at the first sign of disagreement. A great way to rehabilitate criminals, don't you think?

And there was the persecution complex. It was surprising that even the most intelligent convict in there believed that the California Justice System wanted to put people behind bars.

Why? Because of all the money that the prison system generated for the state. The number of employees in the prison system was quite large, so with all the other outside help (food makers, cleaning suppliers, etc.) the CDC industry was a "Billion Dollar industry." These inmates felt that they were only put behind bars because they were victims of a society that thrived and survived by putting men behind bars. Of course, the inmates didn't really belong there. People who were arrested for their 4th DUI shouldn't be there.

Nooo.

They should instead be in a treatment center. They were sick, the poor babies. And drug addicts and dealers, they were the same. They needed treatment, not prison. Basically, these punks felt sorry for themselves, and they couldn't accept the fact that they were ever wrong.

And finally, a convict never makes a mistake, or is wrong about anything, ever! He was always right. That aspect of those assholes really irked me, but I would be leaving too soon to care about it.

Day 317: November 20, 1991

Today, a convict escaped! He was a worker outside the fence at the chicken farm. He was considered a low risk inmate, but I guessed he couldn't handle that shit hole anymore. He was from Yard #6, and that was all I knew. I didn't suppose that they'd catch him!

The twitch in my eye continued as my release date grew nearer.

Day 318: November 21, 1991

I received this from the Lieutenant after "The Hole" incident. Simply put, it set the groundwork for me to have all of my good time reinstated and my Estimated Parole Release Date set to December 12, 1991.

I broke down briefly in the corner of my bed as I read the information. When I needed it most, something good had happened!

CDC-12BG NO.
NAME: GORDAN
Custody: MEB-B   EPRD: 12-12-91
ASSIGNMENT: GRANT "S-TIME" 10-17-91 TO 10-24-91

Comments:
ADMINISTRATIVE ERROR. REASSIGN FAC.V. LT'S CLERK (ASAP) EFFECTIVE 10-1-91 WITH THE APPROPRIATE PAY SCALE FOR THE ASSIGNMENT (3/2).
"G" case was reviewed in absentia this date for a Program Review at the Inmate's request, as the action is non-adverse. Committee's attention is directed to a CDC-128B dated 10-16-91, by Lieutenant, indicating that "G" was placed in AD/SEG on 10-16-91, based upon what was determined as an Administrative error. Therefore, after reviewing the C-file completely, Committee acts to grant "S-time" effective 10-16-91 through 10-24-91. "G" is to be reassigned to the Facility Five Lt's clerk, ASAP, effective 10-16-91, with the appropriate pay scale for the assignment (3/2) effective same date). "G" had previously indicated that he is in agreement with Committee's action this date. "G" 's appeal rights were previously explained. No further action at this time.

DATE: NOVEMBER 20, 1991
INST: ASP CLASSIFICATION

<u>CDC-128-B (Rev. 4/74)</u>
On Wednesday, October 16, 1991, Inmate Gordan, was placed in Administrative segregation because First Watch Staff discovered a letter that he admitted writing, which they viewed to be a threat to another inmate. Upon further review it was determined that Staff totally misinterpreted the contents of the letter and he is no longer deemed a threat to any inmate or to the Safety and Security of this Institution or its Staff. A recommendation has been made that Gordan be released from Administrative Segregation at his initial review.

> Lieutenant
> DATE: October 16, 1991
> A.S.P. GENERAL CHRONO

<u>Day 323: November 26, 1991</u>

On November 25th, I received a message from home that I needed to call home as soon as possible. I figured the call was only in attempts to find out what college courses I would be interested in taking the coming semester. Instead, the news I received was less than pleasing. It was actually quite disturbing.

My mother answered the phone when I called. She told me that the tests had come back from her biopsy, and the results were unfavorable. She had been diagnosed with breast cancer, malignant breast cancer. For some reason, when she told me last week that a bump had been found in her breast, I took it for granted that it would be benign.

Regrettably, I was wrong. I couldn't help but feel responsible for starting the mutation of the cell that was now recognized as cancer. Stress, although not proven to be a cause of cancer, could be the force that starts that first cell to grow irregularly.

And as far as giving out stress levels goes, I'd been the head supplier. I cried a tiny bit that night, to myself of course. A good officer, who I had developed a good relationship with, saw me on my way back from chow and asked me what was wrong. In my attempt to tell him of the situation at home, I almost fell apart. I had to avoid talking to him at that time.

Day 324: November 27, 1991

I was doing much better today. I had talked with an older inmate last night about my trouble. He also could tell something was amiss. He was very helpful in easing the tension I had been feeling since I had talked to my mother. His experience in the death of his parents gave him the wisdom to know how I was feeling at that time, and he was able to tell me a few words that hit home and made me realize that this wasn't the end of the world.

"Everyone is born, and everyone must die," he told me. And he was right. I'd always known it and lived with it, but I also always knew that I would have a hard time when my parents' time to go came along. But he also helped me to come to terms that it may not be as serious as I am making myself believe.

Many women have to have some type of mastectomy. I believe that the statistics are 1 out of 10 women get breast cancer. And many women go on to live a very healthy life after the surgery. The hardest part to accept, and this is probably my mother's area of concern, is the alteration of body image.

I'd be there to help her in this area, though. My nursing education would be helpful in getting my mom to believe that she was normal after the surgery. I loved the lady. She'd done a hell of a lot for me, not just this year, but all of my life. And being in there, I realized that a lot of guys don't get the affection and support from their parents that I have always received from mine. Since I talked with the inmate, I was much more at ease.

My mother was very worried about me after she told me. She thought that I'd do something stupid. But little did she realize that I wasn't as crazy as she thought. I was much more in control of my faculties than she gave me credit for.

I was all right at that point. I didn't feel the tension that she and Gina were afraid I'd experience. I was going to get out of that cesspool, and never look back. As of that day, I had 16 days to go until I went home. I'd be signing my parole papers tomorrow. I overheard them making the list today at my job as a clerk. I should get my "S" time ducat tonight. "S" time is the time given 10 working days before paroling from an institution, in which the facility gathered up your records, cleared out your trust account (used for canteen purchases), and checked to make sure there weren't any holds on you for other crimes. I just wanted out. I knew I was clean!

Day 325: November 28, 1991

It was Thanksgiving Day, and the weather had given me the feeling of the season. It was windy and cold, and it was the way winter should be. I had much to write about, since I was now only fifteen (15) days until my release from that hell hole.

Last night was a bit tense. The ducats that officially change a job for an inmate are usually given out at about 2200 hours. That time came and went without any ducats being passed out. I was expecting to get my Pre-Release Preparation ducat, since I was so close to my time to go home. PRP was the time an inmate quits working, and the institution closes out the inmate's accounts, and completes the necessary paperwork for his release and parole.

Needless to say, since I was less than 10 working days from my release date (due to the four (4) day weekend starting today), I was a little bit distraught.

However, after the shift change, the officers who work at night handed out the ducats and I received my PRP job change. I was quite happy about it, and I slept very well that night, despite all the noise in the housing unit until late hours into the morning.

The late night activity happens on any night before a holiday or weekend day. I found it funny that even in prison, the state encourages people to stay up late. The inmates were allowed to stay up as late as 2:30 in the morning. Since only a few inmates had to report to their job assignments that day, most of the inmates were up all night last night making spreads. A spread was a big pile of noodles, spread out on a plastic bag covering a table, with anything that the inmates participating and eating could contribute to it. The ingredients included crackers, jalepeno peppers, mayonnaise, cheese, beef jerky, and seasonings. It is all thrown into a big pile, except for the crackers, which were used to scoop up the spread contents and shove into one's mouth. I did not participate in any spreads because it was a symbol of "Brother hood", and because the idea of eating a pile of food that looked about as appetizing as the puke of some wino on the sidewalk didn't appeal to me. (I guess I was weird.)

I received good news about my mother's cancer. I talked to my dad, who actually sounded relieved, and my dad usually does not let that sound out. I love the man dearly, but he did hide his emotions, not unlike most men of this world. Anyway, mom's condition was a non-invasive cancer. The doctor that my parents talked to assured them that the cancer would be removed with only a partial mastectomy, and that he was sure that he could eliminate the cancer 100%.

I had made sure I kept away from becoming a peckerwood. A good white boy who would stand up and fight for any other white that needs his help. Most woods had tattoos of swastikas, and "White Pride" all over their bodies, not to mention the naked women that they claimed was an exact replica of' their wives or girlfriends! I just wasn't into the shit these inmates were into. I refused to hate people because of their jobs (cops) and talk like I could whip anyone and everyone in the institution. I was not a macho type of man, and the inmates there were just that.

I looked forward to being back home with each passing day, and I wondered what the parole officer I was assigned to would say upon my release. I'd have to try to keep my head on straight as he went through the regiment of what I had to do while on parole. I only hoped he or she wasn't the type that wanted to throw me back in prison. I had heard many inmates here say that that is all most parole officers want to do, but then I'd remember that these same inmates have the brain capacity of a dung-beetle!

Fifteen days and counting.

Day 327: November 30, 1991

By now, my stay in the "hole" had become the joke of the office. While I was in the hole, I had written a "request for interview" slip to the Lieutenant. In it, I had written,

"Lieutenant, Undoubtedly you have heard of my placement in Ad/ Seg. I have been falsely accused of threatening another inmate. I hope that in working together this past month I have been able to show you what type of person I am. If you believe in me, I would very much like to talk with you, and explain what has happened. I would like to continue working for you if that is at all possible after my release from Ad/Seg. Yours, Respectfully . . ."

I was on my 3rd day in Ad/Seg (which stands for Administrative Segregation) and I was losing hope that this would be dropped and my name cleared. You can imagine how funny it sounded then, after the fact.

Today, I was very busy typing away when the Lieutenant walked in. I was so into what I was typing that I didn't pay attention to what he was saying. Then I heard him say,

"Help me, Help me, I'm locked up in Ad/Seg."

I looked up with a jerk, like I'd just been hit in the back of the head with a brick! He was looking right at me, and all the other clerks were laughing pretty hard. I instantly realized he was mocking that request form I had sent him. I had to laugh, too. If you can't laugh at yourself in this situation, you're in for a hard time!

So, I had a pretty good rizzing from the others, but it was taken lightly, since I can and do laugh at that "hole" episode. (Pun intended)

I'd never hear the end of my stay in Ad/Seg until I left Mountaincrest. The office was always doing the bed moves to and from the "hole," and every time it came up, someone was sure to say something like, "Well, looky here! Somebody's going to the hole. Gordan, tell us what he should expect?"

The Lieutenant called the "hole" Mountaincrest's Hotel Hilton, where they bring the food to your door, you never have to get dressed, and you don't have to worry about your girlfriend being home when you call—because you don't get to use the phone!

Since phone calls were now limited at the prison with the implementation of new rules, I was becoming increasingly anxious over not speaking to Mindy. My anxiety showed in the last letter I wrote, as I wondered if she had moved on to someone else.

Day 336: December 9, 1991

As my time grew very short, the events of the prison just kept getting better. Please note; that's sarcasm.

With two days left of my prison sentence, the entire facility—not just Yard #5, but all of the yards—were on Lock Down due to violence. More crips and bloods crap. I didn't see any violence on our yard, but the reports I heard from the other clerks still working in the office said there was a mess of paperwork to be done. I was glad I was done working and on my 3 day vacation before leaving.

But I was extremely concerned about getting out of there without any altercation taking place between me and the guy I went to the 'hole' over.

121

Apparently, the Sergeant who took me to Adseg had confiscated the radio, and now that inmate was telling me I owed him a new radio. Yeah, that was going to happen.

Today, one of this inmate's friends approached me, significantly bigger than his friend and a bit bigger than myself in build, asking how I was going to make it right.

So we went to a corner of the dorm and I explained to him in detail what had occurred that night and that my intentions were to keep him from getting hurt or worse. I doubt he believed me. The look in his eye was one of disbelief, but I didn't have any altercation since that time through the rest of the night.

The twitch in my eye continued to grow worse. I rubbed it constantly to try to make it stop. Then the guards announced that a windstorm was heading towards the prison, and the yards will remain shut down until it passes. Sounded kind of stupid to me. What the hell's a windstorm going to do anyway?

Day 337: December 10, 1991

Funny what you learn in a prison. A windstorm is more than just a bunch of wind here in the desert. It's a sand storm. Since it was necessary to walk to the chow hall, and the distance you could see was about 10 feet, we were taken in groups of 10, following the walls of the yard, to the chow hall. One of the guards told me to take off my glasses or they'd get sand scratched. He said the windshield on his car was frosted; it was like looking out through the glass in a shower stall with calcium deposits on it!

When my group went outside, it seemed like it was dusk. Very little sunlight was getting through the thick sand clouds that had formed from all of the wind. I'd never seen anything like it before.

I had two days left before freedom, and the events of the past two days had been nerve-wracking.

I hadn't had any words with the inmate with the radio or his friends up to this point, but my friends in here were helping me keep an eye out. One thing on my side is that one of my friends is good friends with one of the radio owner's friends, and they were talking to get the situation all cleared up.

I happened to see the Lieutenant while in the chow hall, and I asked him if there was any chance of getting the radio back to its owner. He said he was planning to return it to him after I departed. By getting the word out that he'd get the radio back after I was gone, the chance of violence against me was decreased.

Just let me out of here and I'd never look back!

Day 338: December 11, 1991

I passed the time as I always had, except with the yard still on lockdown, all 250 inmates of each dorm were inside. This made me uneasy. I had been told that it was not uncommon for a long timer inmate to cause a confrontation with an inmate who was known to be leaving soon, so as to have some time added back on to his stay in Funderland.

I stayed on my bunk or in my dorm the whole day, leaving only to eat breakfast and dinner. Lunch, I decided, wasn't worth the risk of going to the chow hall.

The rest of my day was completely uneventful. I played cards until about 9:30pm and went to bed early. Surprisingly, I did not have trouble falling asleep. The stress of knowing I could be attacked at any moment had me on the alert all day, and when I finally laid down to rest, I couldn't care anymore.

It was 11:00pm when a female guard woke me up. Something was wrong!

"Get dressed, shoes and all," she said, "and report to the guard station.

"Oh crap, what's happening now?" I thought as I rapidly dressed. "It's all over. I'm going back to the 'hole' for some reason. I won't be home for Christmas. Man, I knew it was too good to be true."

I walked up to the guard station in the center of the dormitory, but the guards were not around. I waited patiently until I saw one of the other clerks, this one for a Sergeant, roll up in his wheelchair.

"What the hell's going on?" he asked me. My reply was just as unsure. However, I felt better about the situation.

"If I was a clerk," I thought, "and this guy's also a clerk, then maybe they need something in the office? Nah," I corrected myself, "we must both be in trouble for something that happened on our shifts."

Soon enough the two guards returned to their station and handed both of us passes to the Lieutenant's office. The other inmate asked the guards what was happening, and the female guard barked out, "Go to the Lt.'s office. They'll explain there."

Neither of us had been outside when it was this late, and the spectacular view of stars above us was shockingly clear. The last time either of us had been out was for dinner earlier this evening, only 6 hours ago. At that time, the sand storm still cut the sunlight off from ground level, and the sand had still been blowing around so fast that it hurt the face.

But now, now the wind was gone, the air was clean and cold, and the only traces of the sand storm were the dunes of sand now covering the yard, the asphalt, and the weight pile. The stars above were so bright that I had to stop for a moment to look up.

"Incredible," I thought, "that when you're in the middle of the desert with no city lights shining to diminish the brightness of the stars, how beautiful they can really be."

My amazement was shattered suddenly when a guard outside yelled, "Get your ass in here!"

Once inside the Lt.'s office, the reason for the calling of the Sergeant's clerk and myself became clear. All of the clerks I had worked with while I was the Lt.'s clerk were here. One of the other dormitories had erupted in violence, a spill over of the same violence that shut down the yard a couple of days before.

Only this time, a prisoner was shot and killed.

Roughly 20 inmates were going to the 'hole', and all of them needed the correct forms typed up for their processing. I could type the fastest, so the Sergeant in charge told me to get typing while the other clerks would be doing the filing, sorting, and other support work necessary for such a large transfer of location for inmates.

The work was completed around 2:00am on December 12, 1991. I was to gain my freedom in 7 hours.

Day 339: December 12, 1991

Sleep came easy, and I was up before anyone else in the dorm. Time was flying, and before I was ready with my belongings in a pillowcase, the call came for me to take the walk to the yard gate. As I exited the dorm, the morning sun was brightly shining down, like a small gift from Mother Nature saying, "Remember what you have learned here."

As I walked, I felt like a thousand pound weight had suddenly been lifted from my shoulders. As if the gravity on earth had suddenly decreased from the normal 14 pounds of pressure per square inch to about 11 pounds psi. Nothing really noticeable, but every movement was so much easier.

As I neared the yard gate, the Lieutenant was standing outside. He walked up to me, and for the first and only time during my stay at Mountaincrest, did someone extend his hand to me. I shook his hand firmly, saying "It's been a pleasure working for you."

"I know I won't be seeing you again," he stated. "Whatever your life has in store for you from here on, I know I won't be seeing you again." And with that, he turned and went back into the office.

Already in an emotional state, I was glad I had my sunglasses on, because the tears that welled in my eyes wouldn't go over too well in a state penitentiary, even on my way out!

Each of the other five inmates being released or transferred to another yard were checked for proper ID, the small bag of belongings they had were searched, and the yard gate was opened. The walk from Yard #5 to the release center was about half a mile, and the cool morning air made the walk to freedom that much more enjoyable.

When I arrived at the release center, the clothes that had been sent in by my mother weeks earlier were traded to me for the prison-issued clothing I'd been wearing. After 339 days, I was finally wearing clothes that fit me well. While this may seem like such a trivial matter, when you've experienced all that I had this year, it was a big deal.

My younger brother and sister had driven down to pick me up. The last thing that the guard told me as I was leaving the last barbed-wire fence behind me was "Don't run. The guards in the tower will think you're trying to escape and shoot you." Whether he was serious or just getting one last jibe in at my expense, I walked, albeit quickly, into the parking lot where I saw my siblings waiting. And of course, they started to run towards me!

"Stop running!" I yelled, almost afraid that the guard was serious.

As we left Mountaincrest State Prison behind, I kept my promise to myself and never looked back. I never did get to see what the prison looked like from the low-lying mountain range that surrounded the prison. In fact, I did not stop staring straight ahead until we had reached Coalinga, about a 30 minute drive to the North.

Mindy couldn't be there to pick me up that day. She had to work, and being a new job, it was not possible to ask for the day off. Mindy and I had made plans to meet at my dad's house after she got off work.

After the 4 hour drive home, as I exited the car, my mother met me out front. As with any mother who's son had been exiled for a year, she broke down, sobbing uncontrollably, and I joined her. The taste of freedom was sweet, and I knew at this moment that now came the hard part of getting my life back in order.

❈ Part V: Conclusion

I was released from Mountaincrest State Prison on December 12, 1991. I had been locked up for 339 days. During my incarceration, I witnessed events that I never imagined were the reality of prison life. After my release, I completed my parole 1 year early, gaining early release due to consistent filings with my parole officer, maintaining steady employment, and passing the random drug tests that I was given over the next two years.

I finished the nursing program at CSU, Mountaincrest, graduating in the fall of 1993 with my baccalaureate degree. When I applied to the nursing board to take the nursing board test to become a registered nurse, I was denied the chance to become a nurse due to this conviction. The review board must have really taken time to consider my application, too. They responded within one week. Amazing since the transcripts of the court proceedings sent to them in their entirety (along with the application) were over 500 pages long.

After being denied once, at $400 for the application fee, I never looked back at nursing as a career. Although that was what I wanted to do, it was obvious to me that no one who did not know me personally would ever look past the conviction to see what had actually occurred. That's what the nursing review board did.

And that's what happened with most employers I had in the future. I began working for a temp agency as clerical help. At each temp job I had for the first year and a half after my prison sentence, the employer asked me to become a permanent employee. However, on the application for the job, I was faced with informing the new employer of my conviction, or lying about it and checking 'No' to the question: Have you ever been convicted of a felony?

It took me a long time to find steady employment, but I finally began working for an automotive repair shop that needed a computerized accounting system. Without any prior knowledge of how to make it work, I set up and maintained, for 2 years, an accounting system that kept track of inventory and profits for the four-store chain. It was the beginning of a new career. Computerized bookkeeping.

As for all of the Federal and State assistance programs available to me as an ex-convict, I took advantage of none of them. Despite the hardships that would follow because of my conviction, I would not allow the state or the federal government to treat me like I was special for that conviction. I had been well aware of minorities receiving jobs they were less qualified for than non-minorities simply because of their 'status', and since I didn't agree with that, I wasn't going to be a hypocrite and take advantage of the system for me.

As my dad had told me in his letter to me before my release from Mountaincrest, it was up to me to decide if I would lie to people about the conviction, or if I would tell them the truth.

At first, I decided to tell the tale only to those whom I felt comfortable with. But I noticed that many of the people I told about the incident would suddenly change their opinion of me. They were no longer so friendly. This type of change caused me to stop telling people about my past and make up a lie to hide what had happened to me.

I had done all that I could to avoid the confrontation with Bob that led up to my incarceration. Amazing that it came to this, since I had always been a peacemaker in grade school. And as the years following my release went by, I would have conversations with new friends and coworkers about situations like mine, without letting on that it was I that had actually been involved in such an attack.

I would instead say I "had a friend" that had been involved in the situation that had caused such a large hole in my life.

Most people agreed that they could never hurt another person like the way 'my friend' had; they just couldn't. That was how I felt until I was backed into a corner, where the police were against me, and the only way to get out of the corner was to come out fighting.

I now knew why I was convicted for this crime. No one who hasn't been there can even begin to understand the fear that accompanies it. A life or death situation is rarely encountered in our lifetimes. The ability to imagine what it is like to either kill or be killed is something that civilization has caused us to forget. The American way of debating and verbalizing instead of physical violence has somehow made the public at large incapable of knowing what its like to be threatened and unprotected.

I learned from the incident that took place that the justice system in this country operates illogically. Attorneys can only be wealthier if they consistently win cases (motivational force). However, many defendants are guilty of the crime they are charged with. Being a smart mouthed lawyer can get anyone convicted of a charge (as in my case) and can also get anyone found innocent even when the evidence is very clear that the charged person is guilty.

I hope that someday our justice system is changed, so that people like myself don't get caught up in the system. Many men arrested on false charges like myself never recover, and their lives are ruined.

In my case, the District Attorney knew of the knife found at the hospital in the days after the stabbing between Bob and I, yet he did not fingerprint the knife, knowing that in 9 months when this case went to trial, no prints would be able to be lifted from it. The D.A. wanted to win the case at any expense—even at the cost of my life.

But karma came into play. This D.A. was murdered 6 months after my conviction by his own nephew!

But my attitude towards the judge in my case changed over time. When he threw out the use of the knife, he must have been under the impression that, indeed, the lack of testing the other knife found at the hospital was pure negligence on the part of the D.A., and the judge's decision to throw that part of the case out left me with no doubt that I had been wrong about the judge.

I had always thought he was against me, allowing rulings that were harmful to my case, and not allowing statements that were in my favor. In the end, I came to believe that he did get it. Whether or not I was correct in that assumption is to be decided by each person who reads this story.

Our court system states that we are "Innocent until proven guilty." If that is so, why is the verdict Guilty or Not Guilty? Should not the choice be Guilty or Innocent? I believe that our court system needs to change so that innocent defendants are found "Innocent", and take away the right of lawyers to play with people's lives like bargaining chips.

And I believe this country should stop allowing criminal activity in our society and saying that it is capitalism. The best example I have is the use of licensed contractors in the state of California. You see, in California, unlike most other states, anyone who wants construction work done on their home or property in excess of $300 for both parts and labor must use a licensed contractor.

But if the licensed contractor you use doesn't do the job correctly, or doesn't finish it at all, the state of California will do nothing to see that the consumer is justly refunded the portion not owed to the contractor. The state forces you to use a licensed contractor, but if he or she decides to rip you off, the state won't assist you in any way. That is protection of criminal activity.

Despite the obvious reason I was convicted, one reason that I went to jail for my actions was because I didn't know how to play the justice system. All of the criminals I met while incarcerated knew how to play the system, and they all knew how to get over on the system.

I now know, all too late, that one should take the time to plan for such an event in his or her life. Not that you would ever have to use it, but I didn't think about it either, and the decisions I made after the fact certainly contributed to my conviction.

On that April night in 1990, I never should have left my house. Nor should I have left the side of Bob after the fight. In doing so, I basically allowed Bob the chance to pick up his knife and drive away.

Another error I made was by saying anything to the police, because not only did they omit some of what I said from their report, but they also added words that I never said. Police are human; they make mistakes too. Remember, they can question you without an attorney if they haven't placed you under arrest, and yet anything you say can and still will be used against you in the courts.

As a society ever striving for equality and respect of other's rights, I don't believe we should allow our justice system to continue on the path it has taken over the last 40 years. Changes must be made in the way our prisoners in jails and penitentiaries in this country are treated.

If we are so busy watching out for Prisoner's Rights, we are losing sight of why they were incarcerated in the first place! Prison is prison; there is no reason for inmates to want to be there. When a prisoner says he/she wants to be locked up, it cannot be questioned that it is much too easy for prisoners in the California penal system. Take away yard rights, take away the weight piles, forbid smoking. Let them riot and shoot the rioters dead. Prison is prison, and we need to reinforce that.

When my appeals trial finally came before the appellate court, I was even more disgusted in the justice system of our country than I had been. Despite all of the overlooked evidence and shady dealings between my defense attorney and the D.A., none of that was argued in the appeals court.

I came to find out that a conviction could only be overturned in an appeals court if it is proven that a legal error occurred during (or prior to) the trial proceedings and that error contributed to the conviction.

I was present in the courtroom as my appeals lawyer argued the case for my conviction to be overturned, and as I listened to his argument, in my defense, I couldn't believe what I was hearing.

His speech to the panel of 3 appellate judges was so ridiculous that I would have upheld the conviction on myself if I were one of those judges! This lawyer had nothing to appeal from my case. His argument was so ridiculous that one of the judges actually stated,

"Your arguments are unsupported and without merit."

It has remained my firm belief that this lawyer was nothing but a fraud. If it were possible to sue a lawyer for misrepresentation, I would have. But the fact that the appellate judges did not fine him or reprimand him in any way for his "unsupported and without merit" arguments led me to believe that this happens all the time. Judges, after all, were lawyers before they became judges, and they obviously support a lawyer's right to take money from those that don't realize how the appeals system works.

Since the day of that appellate hearing, I have never spoken to another lawyer on any legal matter. I will never use one again. In my dealings with them during this traumatic time, I learned that they make deals with each other, and prey on those who believe they have been wrongly convicted.

Mindy filed for divorce without using a lawyer by doing just a little research and going to city hall and paying a $50 fee. I have learned since then that even bankruptcy and getting on disability do not require a lawyer, despite the advertisements by attorneys who make such a claim.

I went on to marry Mindy, and at the time this book was completed, we've just celebrated our 20th anniversary. Against all of the bets of my friends and my family, we have made it together, all the while watching so many other couples that didn't stand the test of time.

I have never had any additional contact with the law enforcement community since my parole ended. I was not one of those that the Lieutenant would see again.

He was right about me.

The End

ABOUT THE AUTHOR

Raised in a good household during the 60's and 70's, I had all the chances to make good of his life. A good education, good health, and a good city to grow up in.

It was in 1990 when my life changed forever. Never in trouble with the law, when the event occurred that is the basis for this book, I was unprepared for the reality of what happened next.

In this book you will read what happened for the next 2 years as I saw a part of the world that most don't want to know exists.

I have told my story to others who called me a liar, saying that "those kind of things don't really happen."

Whether you choose to believe what I have written in my book, or not, is up to you.

www.ingramcontent.com/pod-product-compliance
Lightning Source LLC
Chambersburg PA
CBHW051415280526
45785CB00003B/1069